THE BOOK OF SPORTS VIRTUES

❖

10/09

To Kris —
A FUMA DAD AND
FRIEND.
BLESSINGS

PHIL 3:14

ADVANCE PRAISE FOR
THE BOOK OF SPORTS VIRTUES

With all the negatives coming out of the sports world today, Fritz Knapp has given us a refreshing perspective of life's challenges using real-life stories of famous athletes. *The Book of Sports Virtues* will assuredly encourage and inspire the reader to understand what integrity, character and compassion mean whether you're an athlete or a non-athlete. This book is a must-read!

—Barty Smith, former NFL Green Bay Packer runningback

If there's one thing that I'd like to convey to readers of this timely book, it's that athletics gives back far more in benefits than either coaches or players sow in effort. Thanks to Coach Knapp for pointing out these and other important messages.

—Dean Smith, former University of North Carolina
men's basketball head coach

It's easy to give up on a team, player or sport when it's rocked by scandals or ethical messes. But *The Book of Sports Virtues* is refreshing in its study of rock-solid athletic hall-of-famers who also are outstanding human beings. Fritz Knapp's All-Star lineup is made up of winners in life as well. And that's the way it should be.

—Tom Silvestri, publisher, *Richmond Times-Dispatch*

THE BOOK OF SPORTS VIRTUES

Portraits from the Field of Play

Fritz Knapp

Illustrations by Tommy Edwards

PUBLICATIONS

THE BOOK OF SPORTS VIRTUES
Portraits from the Field of Play

by Fritz Knapp

Illustrations by Tom Edwards
Edited by Michael Wilt
Cover Design by Tom A. Wright
Text Design and Typesetting by Patricia A. Lynch

Scripture quotations are from the New Revised Standard Version Bible, copyright © 1989 by the Division of Christian Education of the National Council of the Churches of Christ in the USA. Used by permission.

Published by ACTA Publications, 5559 W. Howard Street, Skokie, IL 60077-2621, (800) 397-2282, www.actapublications.com

Library of Congress Number: 2007942130

ISBN: 978-0-87946-348-9

Printed in the USA by Total Printing Systems

Year 16 15 14 13 12 11 10 09 08
Printing 10 09 08 07 06 05 04 03 02 01

Contents

DEDICATION

꙰

This book is dedicated to my loving parents, Barbara Knapp and the late Frederick Knapp, whose steady nurturing made me who I am; and my patient wife, Lee, and three awesome children, Cheston, Eric, and Stephen. Your devotion to family amazes me.

I would like to acknowledge my three editors, Michael Wilt, Brice Anderson, and my beloved wife, Lee. These folks have helped shape and refine an otherwise roughly hewn work. Many thanks!

Introduction

Their nicknames often seem to point to triumph: The Iron Horse, Captain Clutch, The Dominator, Mr. October, The Rocket, The Sultan of Swat, Air Jordan, Dr. J. But the true stories of many sports stars are much like those of any other human being. We all must, at some time or another, work and strive to overcome trouble, problems and hardship. Most of us do so on a smaller stage—no lights, cameras, announcers, or postgame interviews. But there is much we can learn about how to live our own lives by studying the stories of great athletes who have overcome hard times and adversity.

The main characters in this book are well-known athletes and sports figures, men and women who have overcome personal misfortune through strength of character. Their stories inspire greatness in others. About ten years ago, I began to study athletes and the qualities that made them great. I was interested in more than their athletic abilities, impressive as those are in individuals who have made it to the top of their games. I was especially interested in their *life* abilities, the way they dealt with the variety of setbacks and struggles that all human beings encounter. In my study I read sports biographies by the dozens, and not just those of the most recent superstars. My reading took me as far back as the late 1800s. I found truly captivating accounts of athletes whose attitudes in their weak moments gave them more enduring legacies than they ever would have earned in athletic competition alone. As I entered some difficult personal times, these athletes became my friends and gave me a sense of hope that the struggles in my life would ultimately make me a stronger person.

I can personally identify with each athlete in this book. There is a part of me in every one of their stories. I have battled fatigue, failure and depression like U.S. Open golf champion Ken Venturi. I have had speech difficulties and low confidence like Amos Alonzo Stagg. My body has failed me at different times, as Gertrude Ederle's and Lou Gehrig's bodies failed them. Despite life's downside, though, I have been blessed with a source of strength that comes from deep within my soul and is a wellspring of incredible peace. This well has been fed, in part, by knowing others—some personally and some through their stories—who fought hard to overcome their difficulties. My spirit has risen in the midst of trials, like an eagle in a storm soaring high above the mountains. But it is the Spirit that can turn tragedy into triumph, despair into hope, and defeat into victory. While the crises of life rage, God's abundant grace is most present.

Each chapter in this book identifies a key personality trait demonstrated by a great athlete or sports figure in his or her struggle against adversity. Here you will read, for example, of the compassion of Gale Sayers and Brian Piccolo; the integrity of Arthur Ashe; the persistence of Althea Gibson; the wisdom of Happy Chandler. Through these and other stories, I hope you will find inspiration and a few new friends to help you along life's journey. Get to know these people and you too will hear the lessons they teach. Let them be your mentors. Bring to your life the virtues described in these stories, and bring your own story into clearer perspective. Be true to who God made you—a shining star in a dimming world. As St. Paul wrote, "Adversity produces character, and character produces hope, and hope will not disappoint." Let adversity help turn you into the successful person God has created you to be—a person of hope, a person of character.

APPRECIATION

Lou Gehrig

Baseball, America's national pastime, helps take people's minds off their troubles. In search of someone to lift their spirits, Americans viewed Babe Ruth, the first mighty home-run hitter, as a source of strength. In Ruth's shadow lived a man named Lou Gehrig, whose baseball skills equaled those of the Babe, but whose most noticeable traits were his positive attitude, courage and appreciation. His inner strength outshone even his outstanding baseball career, and his example breathed new life into a nation that was hungry for heroes.

❖❖

Lou Gehrig was born on June 19, 1903 in New York City to German immigrant parents who spoke little English. Mr. Gehrig labored in the sheet metal industry but was often out of work. Mrs. Gehrig worked long, hard hours as a maid and cook to support her family. Lou, having learned the importance of hard work from his parents, held down odd jobs, such as selling newspapers in his neighborhood, to help support his family.

When he wasn't working or studying, he played sports. Mr. Gehrig encouraged his son to play soccer, at which he excelled, and then football. Lou Gehrig's size, strength, and speed gave him a distinct advantage in most sports, but especially football. He starred at running back and kicker. His father was disappointed when Lou began playing baseball because he thought it was not a good use of Lou's athleticism and large body. But Lou Gehrig's baseball talents were immediately evident. At Commerce High School in upper Manhattan, he began to attract professional scouts with his monstrous home runs and high batting average (he batted over .500 in his high school career).

Mr. and Mrs. Gehrig always stressed education over sports. But a sports scholarship to Columbia University enabled their son to get the education they could not afford. Lou chose Columbia over the many schools competing for his baseball and football talents. It was close to home, and his mother worked there. His parents were thrilled and knew that with a Columbia degree Lou would certainly become a successful engineer, fulfilling their most fervent wish for him. Success, however, came in a different form.

Lou Gehrig received an offer he couldn't refuse halfway through his college years. He accepted a lucrative contract with the New York Yankees, which paid him $3,000 annually and a $1,000 bonus. Gehrig gave much of the money to his parents, whose need he thought was greater than his own. Mrs. Gehrig did not like the fact that her son left school early to play baseball, but she certainly enjoyed his emerging fame as well as the security and ease provided by the money.

Lou spent almost two years with the Yankees' minor league affiliate in Hartford, Connecticut, where he struggled at first, and even looked for other jobs, until he realized that baseball demanded his full attention. It took only a few months for Gehrig to begin to perform brilliantly on the field, and owner Jacob Ruppert, who had spent a fortune to acquire Babe Ruth from the Red Sox in 1918, was quick to see his star-quality talent. Gehrig wore Yankee pinstripes for the first time in 1923, but he did not break into the starting lineup until 1925. When he did, he broke in for good, and Ruth and Gehrig, batting third and fourth in the order, formed the backbone of a team whose hitters became widely known as "Murderer's Row" for their cruelty to opposing pitchers.

But as good as Gehrig and his teammates were, they played second fiddle to the Babe in popularity. In 1927, Gehrig had better overall statistics than Ruth (.375 average, 47 home runs, 175 runs batted in), but Ruth stole the spotlight by hitting a record 60 home runs. Ruth grabbed more press in other ways, too. With his flamboyant lifestyle (he wore big fur coats and smoked cigars) he received much more attention than that quiet Gehrig.

Besides having great individual statistics and winning the Most Valuable Player award in 1927, Gehrig contributed, according to one of his coaches, "dignity and high resolve" to a team that won over 100 games and swept the Pirates 4-0 in the World Series. His manager, Joe McCarthy, called Lou "an influence to the entire team."

When the Great Depression began in 1929, the Yankees as a team were still peaking, even though the mighty Babe Ruth's career was waning. In the 1930s, the Yankees were still youthful and aggressive. From 1932 to 1939 they made it to the World Series five times, and won all five. In the midst of all this success, Lou Gehrig married Eleanor Twitchell, a Chicagoan, in September 1933. Not coincidentally, he had his best year statistically in 1934 and won the Triple Crown for the best batting average, most home runs, and most runs batted in. His devotion to baseball, demonstrated by his streak of consecutive games played, which at the time stood around 1,500, was surpassed only by his loyalty to Eleanor.

Gehrig became the Yankees' captain and their "Iron Horse." He commanded his teammates' respect and returned it with his own. Pitcher Waite Hoyt said, "If I ever have a son, I want him to be just like Gehrig." Lou was described as the "protector of the Yankee image," and he was the "genuine article." As much as he could, he played pick-up baseball games with kids in his Riverdale, New York, neighborhood, and became the sport's foremost role model. No one could have imagined the turn of events that would soon follow.

❦

The 1938 season began routinely, with Lou Gehrig in the starting lineup at first base. He reached the milestone of 2,000 consecutive games played, but his batting average and fielding were decidedly not Gehrig-like. It was the first full season that he failed to bat over .300, and he seemed to lack his usual strength and mobility. Fans and sportswriters called it a slump, and everyone, especially Gehrig, sought a solution.

As poorly as Lou Gehrig finished the '38 season, the worst was yet to come. Attempts in the offseason to discover a cause for his sudden slump were unsuccessful, but he started the 1939 season with high hopes that he could regain his old form. It did not happen. His play worsened. He rarely hit the ball, and when he tried to run, he stumbled and sometimes fell flat on his face.

Gehrig begged Joe McCarthy to take him out of the lineup for the good of the slumping Yankees. McCarthy wouldn't do it. He reasoned that Gehrig's leadership more than offset his poor performance. Besides, he had the utmost respect for Gehrig, and hated the idea of removing him.

Finally, out of sheer frustration, Lou Gehrig pulled himself out of the lineup on May 2, 1939. Fourteen years and 2,130 games had elapsed since his consecutive-game streak began. It was a somber day for all Yankees and their fans. Eleanor, his wife, stepped in to find answers. The first person she called was renowned Chicago physician Dr. Charles Mayo. He did a thorough physical examination and discovered something unexpected. He found that Gehrig suffered from a rare hereditary disease known as amyotrophic lateral sclerosis, or ALS. This disease normally causes widespread muscular paralysis, which explained Gehrig's symptoms. Eleanor learned that ALS is often fatal, but she kept that fact from her husband. Gehrig knew, though, that he would never play baseball again.

Shortly after the news of Gehrig's illness became public, Yankee management arranged a "Lou Gehrig Appreciation Day." A sell-out crowd of some 60,000 gathered on July 4, 1939, to pay tribute to their hero. Players, both teammates and admiring opponents, gave him gifts and praised his example.

Babe Ruth, who had played his last game for the Yankees in 1934 and retired in 1935, spoke at the event, praising his former teammate. When Ruth finished, Gehrig knew it was his turn to speak. Ruth coaxed the reluctant Gehrig to the microphone. Choking back tears, Gehrig delivered what became known as his farewell address, a speech that has been quoted innumerable times ever since:

Fans, for the past two weeks you have been reading about a bad break I got. Yet today I consider myself the luckiest man on the face of the earth. I have been in ball parks for seventeen years, and have never received anything but kindness and encouragement from you fans.

Look at these grand men. Which of you wouldn't consider it the highlight of his career just to associate with them for even one day?

Sure I'm lucky. Who wouldn't consider it an honor to have known Jacob Ruppert; also the builder of baseball's greatest empire, Ed Barrow; then to have spent six years with that wonderful little fellow, Miller Huggins; then to have spent the next nine

*years with that outstanding leader, that smart student of psy-
chology—the best manager in baseball today, Joe McCarthy?*

*Sure, I'm lucky. When the New York Giants, a team you
would give your right arm to beat, and vice versa, sends you a
gift—that's something.*

*When you have a wonderful mother-in-law who takes sides
with you in squabbles against her own daughter—that's something. When you have a father and mother work all their lives
so that you can have an education and build your body—it's a
blessing! When you have a wife who has been a tower of strength,
and shown more courage than you dreamed existed—that's the
finest I know.*

*So I close in saying that I might have had a tough break; but
I have an awful lot to live for.*

Gehrig's show of appreciation for his family and friends gave all
Americans a glimpse of his generous character, his quiet strength, and
his inner peace. When he died on the evening of June 2, 1941, less than
two years after his famous speech, Eleanor was at his side. She described
his expression at the moment of his death as "peace beyond description.
A thing of ecstatic beauty, and seeing [it] we were awestricken and even
reassured. We did not cry. We seemed stronger, and not one of us left
that room without feeling: There is a better place than this. Wherever it
is, no tears, no tyrant."

Cultivating Appreciation

Our purpose is to cultivate in the largest possible number of our future citizens an appreciation of both the responsibilities and the benefits which come to them because they are Americans and are free.

—John Bryant Conant (Harvard University President, 1943)

Facts of the Matter
ALS Today

Amyotrophic lateral sclerosis is literally synonymous with Lou Gehrig—ALS is known far and wide as "Lou Gehrig's Disease." It remains incurable, but doctors have found new ways to treat it so that strength and mobility can be better managed for longer periods of time. Pitcher Curt Schilling, a future Hall of Famer, and his wife, Shonda, have taken up the cause of battling ALS. Though they have no family members with ALS, the Schillings were so impressed by the character and courage of an ALS patient they met when Schilling was pitching for the Philadelphia Phillies that they started Curt's Pitch for ALS. Find out all about it at www.curtspitch.org.

COMPASSION

Gale Sayers and Brian Piccolo

The debate over equal rights for members of all races divided America in the 1960s. Some white Americans wanted to keep the races separate and unequal; many fought for equality. By the 1960s, African Americans had been playing professional football for decades, but as the number of black players increased in the National Football League, many Americans watched closely to see if the league's policy for integrating players of different races would take effect peacefully.

❖·❖

Gale Sayers and Brian Piccolo were teammates with the Chicago Bears in the 60s. Sayers was black and Piccolo was white. They were also roommates, and as they became friends they also grew to appreciate each other's differences. They learned that friendship and helping others could transcend the reality of race. Most importantly, they shared deeply in each other's joys and sorrows, and in the process showed many Americans that a friend's love stretches far beyond the color of his skin.

Gale Sayers and Brian Piccolo were both All-American college football players as seniors in 1964. Sayers, a lightning-fast University of Kansas running back nicknamed the "Kansas Comet," dazzled football fans across the United States. He broke many Kansas rushing records during his four-year career and many professional teams eagerly sought after him. Piccolo, from Wake Forest University in Winston-Salem, North Carolina, was also a running back. He distinguished himself by gaining the most yards and scoring the most points in the entire country. He

23

was known for his tough running, and often ran straight into—rather than around—defenders. Piccolo's records did not impress the NFL, whose scouts thought that his straight-ahead running style would not work well at the highest football level. Besides, they figured, he was only six feet tall and weighed under 200 pounds, not the size for pushing around much bigger defensive linemen.

When the NFL held its 1965 draft, Gale Sayers was picked first by the Chicago Bears of the National Football League. He had a hard decision to make, because another team in the newer, rival American Football League, the Kansas City Chiefs, wanted him as well. Because the NFL had a well-established reputation and better financial security, Sayers decided to sign with the Bears.

Brian Piccolo, on the other hand, was not drafted by a professional team. It seriously dampened his dream of playing professional football and left him with the option to try out for a team as a free agent at summer training camp. The Bears were the one team willing to give Piccolo a chance to prove that he was capable of playing with the "big boys." In training camp drills and scrimmages, he impressed the coaches with his intensity and all-around play: running, blocking, and catching passes. After watching Piccolo perform close up, the coaches decided he was valuable enough to keep on their roster. Having used all the determination he could muster, Brian Piccolo achieved the first step toward his dream of playing in the NFL.

Although they were now teammates, Sayers and Piccolo had little in common. Sayers quickly became first-string running back because of his break-away speed and touchdown-scoring potential. Piccolo, sidelined with a nagging hamstring injury, could only cheer him on. But Piccolo quickly developed into a first-rate encourager, a person who readily talked openly and honestly to his teammates. He also made them laugh with his sharp wit. A former Wake Forest teammate, Bill Faircloth, said about Piccolo: "He'd always have some kind of practical joke going.

[Wake Forest] lost eighteen in a row at one point and times were hard, but Brian was one of those happy-go-lucky guys, and he always had a joke or something to keep us loose." His upbeat attitude had the same effect on the Bears.

The climax of Gale Sayers' season was being named Rookie of the Year. He overwhelmed all other rookies in the voting. Piccolo received no such praise, but his role on the Bears as an inspirational leader stood out more than his play. By joking with his teammates and pushing them to do their best, he won their friendship and respect.

Gale Sayers and Brian Piccolo drew closer as players in 1966. The Bears' lockers were arranged in numerical order. Sayers and Piccolo prepared for games right next to each other. Confident in his abilities after his injury-plagued rookie season, the Bears placed Piccolo as back-up running back to Sayers. Piccolo was perfect in this role, because his encouragement pushed Sayers to perform at his best. Sayers responded by leading the NFL that year in rushing and by breaking four Chicago Bears' records in the process. He also established the league record for the most yards gained in a single season (2,440). Brian Piccolo couldn't have been happier for his teammate, even though his own playing time was limited.

In 1967 the Bears coaching staff made the controversial decision of rooming Sayers and Piccolo together for road games. This small decision by the Bears shocked many people, because it was the first time in team history that a room pairing was integrated. Neither Piccolo nor Sayers objected, though, because they had become friends the previous season. When asked about it by reporters, Piccolo mostly joked about being put together with Sayers. Sayers, in turn, joked about having been assigned Piccolo as a roommate. Their calmness in discussing black-white integration helped reduce any public controversy the decision had created. When people saw how easily Piccolo accepted Sayers, and vice versa, they were somewhat surprised. It brought a ray of hope that the two worlds, black and white, could draw together, both in football and throughout American society.

Such was not the world in which Piccolo and Sayers grew up. As youths, they knew little about the other's world. American life was rigidly segregated in the 1940s and '50s, especially in the Deep South where Piccolo grew up. The Midwest, where Sayers was raised, had more racial mixing but not nearly equal treatment. Blacks and whites were taught in most communities to stick to their own race, and whites often maintained an attitude of superiority.

Gale Sayers was born in 1943 in Wichita, Kansas. He was the middle of three sons born to Roger and Bernice Sayers, who were native Midwesterners. His father Roger had grown up in Speed, Kansas, on 360 acres in the northwestern agricultural part of the state. Bernice Ross Sayers was originally from Texas, but her family settled in Wichita when she was a young girl. Roger Sayers was a talented athlete. He had great speed, a trait his sons Roger Jr. and Gale would inherit, and was well-suited for many sports. Baseball and track were his favorites. He also was a fine piano player. He played both the piano and baseball semi-professionally (part-time and for money).

Roger and Bernice Sayers' first two children, Roger Jr. and Gale, were born within thirteen months of each other, in April 1942 and May 1943. Ronnie, their last child, was born in 1948. Mr. Sayers worked for Goodyear Tire and Rubber Company as a mechanic and earned a good salary, which in those days was around $50 a week. He disciplined his children firmly, but his strictness made his boys understand that their attitudes and behavior mattered most to their parents. Roger and Bernice did their very best to channel their sons' energies into the most appropriate outlets. Sports became the activity of choice, for both the parents and the children.

Life for the Sayers, while relatively prosperous in Wichita, began a slow but steady decline when the family moved several hundred miles to Speed, Kansas, in 1950. Roger's father, a wheat farmer, had become ill, and he requested that his son come home to tend the farm. Roger, out of respect, obliged his father

and moved his family, much to the chagrin of Bernice, whose family still lived in Wichita. A general feeling of unhappiness and loneliness settled upon Bernice, and the sixteen months they spent in Speed before Roger's father died were sheer misery for her. She began to drink alcohol excessively to escape the pain that living in an unfamiliar town caused her. After Roger's father died, the family moved to Omaha, Nebraska. Bernice's alcoholic binges became routine, and she would leave her family for weeks at a time and return to Wichita. Roger coped well in her absence, feeding and raising three growing boys on his own. But he, too, began drinking too much, only compounding an already bad situation for Gale and his brothers.

In Omaha, the five Sayers first lived with Roger's brother, Guy, because it was the only arrangement Roger could afford at the time. Two families living in a two-bedroom house lasted only two months. When Roger found work in Omaha as a car polisher, he was able to move his family into the local "projects," apartments where other low-income families lived.

On the job, he became what one car dealer called "the best in the city" at making cars shine. He would spend much of his $65-a-week salary, however, on drinking or gambling. The Sayers couldn't pay their bills and wound up moving nine times in eight years, each time to a worse neighborhood. Ghetto life, in the dirtiest and most overcrowded housing, became the Sayers' standard living conditions.

Games in the streets as well as organized little leagues made life more fun and bearable for the Sayers boys. They had grown accustomed to being poor, which included wearing ragged clothes and eating inadequate meals such as chicken claws. They turned their physical hunger into competitive drive and made the most of a bad situation. Young Gale took full advantage of the organized football leagues that Omaha offered.

Gale Sayers excelled on the athletic field while still in grade school. Besides playing baseball, basketball and running track, Gale's favorite sport was flag football. Many of the teams for which Gale played won city championships. Roger Jr. and Gale made a dynamic tandem as teammates, because both had blazing speed. As a freshman at Central High School in Omaha, Gale was a meager 110-pound running back, but he helped lead his team to its first freshman championship in twenty-three years. The next year, Roger and Gale were paired on Central High's varsity team. Roger's quick moves and ability to gain big yardage made him the best running back in the city that season, his junior year. Gale's running suffered that season. He had trouble maneuvering his body with the fifty pounds of added muscle he had developed while cutting grass the previous summer. The additional weight eventually helped him avoid injury and challenge larger opponents.

Roger Jr. and Gale also excelled at track. After winning state titles in the 100-yard and 220-yard sprints, both sophomore and junior years, Roger had over a hundred college scholarship offers to run track. Gale took longer to develop in track, but in his senior season he won state-wide gold medals in the low hurdles, 880 relay, and the long jump, which at 24 feet 11¾ inches, set the Nebraska high school record. These feats, combined with an undefeated and record-breaking football season in which he scored 108 points, put Gale in contention for the Nebraska "Athlete of the Year." He was narrowly beaten out by another track and football star, Kent McCloughan, who went on to become a defensive back with the Oakland Raiders.

The Sayers household became a recruiting ground for colleges. Roger Jr. accepted a track scholarship to Omaha University, where he had an outstanding career (even beating Bob Hayes, the eventual 100-yard dash world record holder and "fastest man in the world"). Gale also had many scholarship offers. He narrowed his final decision to the University of Nebraska and the University of Kansas, football power-houses in the states where he had lived. He liked both coaches and both campuses, but in the end decided on Kansas for the better opportunities he thought it would give him to play professional football. Some of his Nebraskan peers resented his decision, and the seeming disloyalty to their state. But Gale Sayers' dreams of an NFL career prevented him from any second-guessing.

Gale Sayers was painfully shy in high school. He talked little, and when he did, he was difficult to understand. He had what a friend described as a "lazy tongue." Poor speech made social interaction awkward for Sayers, who did his best not to reveal his weakness. His schoolwork also suffered from his language handicap and general lack of motivation.

Linda, his girlfriend, helped him improve his attitude toward school and life in the sports spotlight.

Linda Bullard, from Omaha, was a student at Omaha Tech, Central High's archrival, when she and Gale met during his junior year. They dated each other throughout high school, and Gale soon realized he felt completely relaxed around Linda. She felt needed, something that she lacked from her upbringing (she was the fifth of five children and often felt overlooked). They helped each other overcome childhood deficiencies, and before graduating from high school they were engaged to be married.

Going away to college was one of the toughest things Gale Sayers had done up to that point in his life. He felt lonely and unhappy being apart from Linda. Schoolwork demanded more of him than it had in high school. To cope with the academic strains, he began to cheat on exams. One blatant cheating attempt, caught by a suspicious professor, brought disciplinary action. A failing grade and stern warning only deterred Sayers slightly. A desperate feeling caused him to keep cheating. He tried to make passing grades any way he could, even if it meant breaking the rules.

Gale Sayers merely survived in the classroom, but he thrived on the football field. He starred on Kansas' freshman team and showed the varsity coaches that his running could carry them a long way. Sayers' homesick freshman year ended on a high note when he married Linda in June. Marital bliss was just the cure he needed.

While Linda brought joy into Gale Sayers' life, the influence of two men at the University of Kansas gave his life new direction and focus. First, his track coach, Bill Easton, taught him lessons about priorities and working hard. Coach Easton, a highly respected coach, had a sign on his desk that read: I AM THIRD. Curious, Sayers asked his coach what the sign meant. Easton replied, "It means the Lord is first, my friends [and family] are second, and I am third." This saying was packed with meaning for the coach, but it also forced his standout runner to reflect on his own priorities. Gale Sayers adopted this phrase as his own life philosophy. His new mindset gave the most significant people in his life the focus they deserved from him. It liberated Sayers from a purely selfish attitude.

The other man who dramatically affected Gale Sayers was an adviser at Kansas named Jesse Milan. He taught Gale how to overcome his speech impediment. He took Gale with him many times when he spoke publicly, at his church or on campus. Jesse became Gale's mentor, and Sayers soaked up the attention. It gave him the boost he needed in college, and his grades dramatically improved. Said Sayers in his 1970 autobiography, *I Am Third*:

> *Well, I did feel more at home with myself. I had a long way to go, I knew, but I was feeling more secure and more self-confident. The contacts I had made, the different people I got close to who worked on me all helped. I think there may have been an explosion inside after all, because I was now aware of my potential—as a football player and as a person.*

Sayers improved himself socially and academically, but it was his football prowess that captured the attention of Kansas fans and football fans across the nation. Three years of running like the wind for the Kansas varsity gave him the recognition he needed for an NFL career: He was a two-time All-American, was named to the All-Big Eight; had Big Eight career and single-game rushing records (2675 yards and 283 yards), and made the longest run from the line of scrimmage in NCAA history (99 yards). As exceptionally as he performed, though, Sayers alone couldn't carry the University of Kansas to a Big Eight championship. The best record Kansas had during his career was 7–3, his senior year. One of the most dramatic moments in Sayers' collegiate career came in the middle of his senior year when Kansas upset Oklahoma 15-14, with Sayers scoring on a 93-yard run. Unfortunately, Kansas lost later that season 14-7 to Nebraska, and the hopes of a Big Eight championship crumbled.

◆-◆

Brian Piccolo was born the same year as Gale Sayers, on October 31, 1943. His mother, Irene, was first-generation American and of German-Hungarian parentage, and his father, Joseph Sr., was a native Italian. Irene and Joseph Piccolo settled originally in Pittsfield, Massachusetts, in the western, mountainous part of the state. There all three of their sons—Joseph Jr., Don and Brian—were born. Mr. Piccolo worked hard as a bus driver, and eventually started his own driving school. This new industry in the 1940s gave Mr. Piccolo a golden opportunity. He earned a good living for his family, one that enabled them to spend the winters in Florida, avoiding the harshest cold weather in the Berkshire Mountains. When their middle son, Don, was stricken with a severe respiratory ailment that caused bleeding from his nose and mouth, the doctor advised the family to remain in the warmer, more humid conditions of southern Florida year-round. Brian was three years old when Mr. Piccolo sold his business interests in Massachusetts and moved the family to Florida.

Brian Piccolo's life revolved around sports. In early grade school he played football, basketball and baseball. In baseball, his best sport, he gained the nickname "Little Yogi" (after Yogi Berra, the New York Yankees' star catcher). Brian's brother Don was also an athlete. Mrs. Piccolo, thrilled with her sons' athleticism, was their biggest fan. She attended most of their games, while Mr. Piccolo worked hard to start another driving school. He later decided it was time to sell the school, and opened a restaurant. He provided well for his family financially, but working long hours meant that he missed his boys' activities.

Growing up in Florida in the 1950s and '60s meant living in a segregated community. Blacks were treated by many whites as second-class citizens. Even more rigidly than in Kansas or Nebraska where Sayers grew up, the social code of the South kept blacks separated from much of white culture, except in inferior roles. The idea of civil rights was adamantly rejected by white political leaders. Schools in the South usually were racially divided (whites attended one school, blacks a different school). Central Catholic, Brian Piccolo's parochial high school, was no exception.

Brian Piccolo's high school experience paralleled Sayers' in a number of ways. First, sports held his attention more than other activities. Piccolo starred in three sports, and although he chose to play football in college, he had opportunities to play professional baseball after high school. Sports, in a real sense, kept him out of trouble, as it had Sayers. They both had friends who could have pulled them in the wrong direction toward activities that were destructive. They had high school coaches who saw vast potential in them and motivated them to progress in sports as much as they possibly could. Central Catholic football coach Jim Kurth saw "great determination—unbelievable determination" in Piccolo. Much of Sayers' motivation came from within himself as well.

Next, both Piccolo and Sayers grew up in a world where whites and blacks did not interact in society all that much. Though Sayers went to a high school that was roughly ninety percent white, he stuck closely to friends from his neighborhood, the Omaha ghettos. Piccolo knew few blacks (he did not have a black teammate until he got to the Bears). Neither fully appreciated the other's race.

Finally, a girlfriend named Joy Murrath, who attended a rival school, factored significantly into Brian Piccolo's high school experience. Piccolo, or "Pic" as his friends called him, spent much time with Joy's family, especially because both his older brothers had moved away from home and his parents worked long hours at the restaurant. Piccolo paid special attention to Joy's sister, Carol, who had cerebral palsy, a physically debilitating disease. She moved about in a wheelchair, and Piccolo's devotion to her included taking her places such as his football games, where she otherwise wouldn't have gone. Carol brought out Brian Piccolo's tender-hearted nature. Joy admired Brian's patience with Carol, and Brian became part of the Murrath family.

Brian was a strong high school football player, but his small size (6 feet, 185 pounds) and average speed as a running back did not impress most college coaches. But his positive attitude and hard work stood out. Whatever he did on the field, whether blocking, running, or catching passes, he did well. Late in his high school senior year, he was awarded an athletic scholarship (the only one he received) to Wake Forest University in Winston-Salem, North Carolina. Though a professional baseball career remained a distinct possibility, he wanted to play college football. He even looked far ahead to playing in the NFL after college. As it turned out, Wake Forest in the early 1960s was not the best place to showcase his talents to NFL scouts. Wake Forest struggled to win games under coach Billy Hildebrand, a fine gentleman but his four years as Wake's head coach produced only seven victories. New head coach Jim Tate arrived prior to Piccolo's senior year.

Coach Tate was a fierce, fiery competitor, and he brought out the best in the team he inherited. His strict discipline during practices caused some scholarship players to quit, but that was part of his overall strategy. He wanted only the toughest, most dedicated players on his team. He won Brian Piccolo's respect early on, and Piccolo caught the coach's eye with his enthusiastic play. Coach Tate gave Piccolo every opportunity to run the ball, and he ran exceptionally well, for many yards and touchdowns. When the season was over, Brian Piccolo led the nation in rushing (1,044 yards) and scoring (111 points), and Wake had finished with a respectable 5–5 record. NFL scouts had begun to look at him as a bona fide "prospect." So confident was Piccolo about his NFL chances that he commented to his best friend, Dan Arnold, "I don't see how I can keep from making a pretty nice bundle next year. I know I sure could use it being married and all that."

Brian Piccolo had married Joy Murrath on December 26, 1964. Interestingly, the postseason Shrine All-Star football game in which Brian played (at this game, he met Sayers for the first time) put a serious kink into their plans. Piccolo was unable to attend his own wedding rehearsal, much to Joy's disappointment. His comment to Joy after arriving via airplane in time for the wedding displayed his quick wit: "You know I hate to practice." His marriage to Joy also revealed Brian's compassionate nature in a special way. When he became engaged to Joy, he gave her a large diamond ring. But he also gave her sister, Carol, a diamond ring as well (although a smaller one). Brian wanted Carol to feel included, as opposed to the way that her cerebral palsy made her feel excluded from many facets of life.

❧❧

With college behind him and settled into his marriage, Piccolo eventually made the Chicago Bears football team at a free agent tryout. As the team's second running back, he backed up Gale Sayers as Sayers excelled at the game and set NFL records. In their second season with the Bears, Piccolo and Sayers became the first interracial pair of players on the team to be assigned to room together when the team traveled.

In his recollections of getting to know his new roommate, Piccolo gave a blunt assessment of what it was like to room with Sayers, and how they were "forced" to spend time together, even though neither had any major objections to the situation:

> *Gale and I got acquainted our second year. We lockered according to numbers: forty, Sayers; forty-one, Piccolo; forty-five, Dick Gordon. I used to tell them [that] they made me feel like an Oreo cookie.*

When they made us roommates, we were forced to spend more time together. We roomed together three years, sixty-seven, sixty-eight, and sixty-nine. At first we did not go out to eat together. When we'd get to a town, I'd call Ralphie or someone, and he'd call the guys he'd been hanging out with, and we'd split. Then we took to going out in a big integrated bunch. Eventually, it got to where Gale and I would always go out together, kind of rely on one another, you know. We'd talk about the game, individuals, most everything.

Sayers remembered that his relationship with Piccolo was first and foremost practical. He relied on Piccolo to help him play through a game without getting totally exhausted. Piccolo helped Sayers maximize his efforts on the field.

I had to get friendly with him because he was my backup man and I needed him. When I was tired I depended on him for a [breather]. He always said, 'I have the distinction of never being put into a game by a coach.' We always worked it between ourselves. Mr. Halas was head coach then and he never liked to take me out of a game. But there were times when I just ran and ran and ran and I was completely whipped. And Piccolo knew it....

Over the next few years, Sayers' relationship with Piccolo evolved, and he reflected on that change in his autobiography:

I guess I was a little distant that first year. I think once people get to know me I'm easy to get along with. Pic always knew that on the day of a game I liked to be left alone—just let me be—and this is what he did. But by the end of that first year we had both loosened up quite a bit.

I think he actually helped open me up because he was such a happy-go-lucky guy. He always had a joke or two in him.

Only a huge star makes All-Pro his first three seasons in the NFL, a feat Sayers accomplished in 1965, '66 and '67, earning his nickname "Magic." His fourth season began with more of the same running brilliance, but the star seemed to flicker with only five games remaining in the season. In a game against the San Francisco 49ers, Sayers was hit hard on a routine running play by San Francisco defensive back Kermit Alexander. The hit was clean but hard, and Sayers' right knee bent in the wrong direction. He felt pain immediately and knew something was drastically wrong. After taking X-rays the Bears' team physician confirmed his worst fear: torn ligaments. He scheduled an operation to repair the damaged knee. Sayers' season ended badly, and he wept tears of frustration and disappointment over this unfortunate turn of events. Making All-Pro for a fourth consecutive year in his injury-shortened 1968 season helped give him an emotional lift. He needed a boost to help him get through the lengthy and torturous rehabilitative program that followed surgery. He had no guarantees that he would recover completely or even play football again.

Sayers' misfortune meant that Piccolo took his place and became the Bears' starting running back for the first time in his career. He wasted no time in proving that he was an able replacement. He gained over 100 yards in total offense (running and pass catching) against the Atlanta Falcons in his first start and finished with 450 yards rushing in the last six games of the season. His quarterback, Jack Concannon, summarized the emotional boost Piccolo's insertion into the Bears' starting lineup gave him:

You couldn't really say Pic could run, but he always did the job. Being a football player and saying it was pleasant to work with someone sounds, well, freaky. But it was the truth. When I'd call a play where the ball would go to Brian, you could see the grin come over his face. He'd look at me—and it was beautiful.

Piccolo's enthusiasm rubbed off on his quarterback and the rest of the team. It inspired them to come miraculously within one point of making it into the NFL playoffs. Piccolo accepted nothing short of excellence from himself and from his teammates.

Although Piccolo benefited from Sayers' injury by getting more playing time, he felt badly for his wounded roommate. He suffered along with him, and when Sayers' rehabilitation therapy began, Piccolo made it his mission to spur Sayers on to a full recovery. He worked out with Sayers during the offseason and persistently encouraged him to press through the physical and emotional pain he felt. Piccolo said afterward:

> *I knew he'd come back after the knee, mostly because of the way he worked it during the offseason. I never saw a guy so determined to get a thing back in shape.... Gale persuaded himself he was one hundred percent.*

His temporary mission completed, Brian Piccolo resumed his backup role to Sayers as the 1969 season began. Without resentment, Piccolo kept pushing Sayers to work hard and regain the quick, sharp-cutting running style he had before the injury. Sayers said in his autobiography:

> *[Piccolo] was a comfort to me during the 1969 exhibition season and into the regular season, especially those early games when the writers had written me off. He was one of the few guys who seemed to have confidence in me, who built up my morale. He would read what they were saying about me and he'd say, "Don't worry about them. You're running fine. The holes aren't there, you know, just keep your chin up."*

It was tough going for all the Bears that year—they struggled all season and won just a single game, finishing with a 1–13 record. But Sayers was a highlight, and his comeback, despite the poor performance of his team, was nothing short of miraculous. He led the NFL in rushing, with more than 1,000 yards. His critics and doubters were silenced. But something gloomy occurred near the end of the season to mute his celebration. During a game against the Atlanta Falcons, Brian Piccolo took himself out because he couldn't catch his breath. Piccolo's toughness had convinced the Bears coaches to play him with Sayers and not behind him, but Piccolo knew he couldn't help the team if he were sickly. He had had a persistent cough most of November, but he thought the cold conditions in Chicago were to blame. To be on the safe side, Piccolo went to the hospital the following week to have X-rays of his chest taken. The X-rays revealed a lump in his chest that later proved to be a malignant tumor. Piccolo's cough was a symptom of a serious disease: lung cancer.

Joy Piccolo was filled with dread when doctors told her the news, but Brian had a different reaction. "Don't cry," he said. "You gotta bounce up. It's a league rule."

Piccolo prepared to fight his condition with every ounce of strength—physical, mental and emotional—that he had. And, of course, Gale Sayers and his teammates would be available to help pick him up, much as he had done for them over the previous three-and-a-half seasons.

Piccolo flew to New York to allow the best surgeons in the world to perform surgery on the tumor. His surgeon, Dr. Ted Beattie, turned out to have been a college football player himself and was a huge Bears fan. When Piccolo arrived at Memorial Sloan-Kettering in New York City, he was more nervous than he had ever been on the football field. But he likened the surgery to a weapon, and the surgeon to a warrior, about to fight his arch enemy—cancer. Those thoughts helped to calm him.

Another big boost to Piccolo's spirits were the calls and mail he received from his coaches and fans all across the country, including owner and former head coach George Halas and celebrities such as Frank Sinatra. Piccolo had become a celebrity himself. When George Halas called Gale Sayers to tell him the seriousness of Piccolo's condition, Sayers was shocked. Halas thought it would be appropriate for Sayers to break the news to his teammates. Sayers agreed. Just prior to their game against Baltimore on Sunday, November 23, Sayers, who at one point in his life hardly could put a sentence together, tearfully shared these words with his team family:

> *Brian Piccolo is very, very sick. If you don't know it, you should know it. He might not ever play football again. And I think each of us should dedicate ourselves to try to give our maximum efforts to win this ballgame and give the game ball to Pic. We can all sign it and take it to him.*

Many in the locker room cried. Sayers couldn't hold his emotions back, even after they had left the locker room and listened to the singing of the national anthem. The game was anticlimactic. They lost it in the fourth quarter, as the powerful Colts, directed by quarterback Johnny Unitas, were simply too strong. Sayers, swept up in the emotion of the game, forgot to get the game ball for Piccolo, something his still-feisty Italian friend Piccolo kidded him about.

The surgeon removed a grapefruit-sized tumor, much larger than expected, from Piccolo's lung. Doctors treated the area in his lungs with both radiation and chemotherapy to combat the spreading cancer. But signs indicated the disease already had spread into his lymph nodes, which did not bode well for Piccolo. Ever the optimist, Piccolo held out hope that he would return to football when the therapy was complete. That December, Brian and Joy Piccolo basked in the celebration of their fifth wedding anniversary and the first birthday of their third daughter, Kristi. Though a dose of chemotherapy left him feeling physically wasted, his spirits soared with his family surrounding him.

The coming months brought the appearance of normalcy to the Piccolo household, as Brian went through training to recover the stamina and muscle he had lost through his lung operation. The girls and Joy enjoyed having more time to spend with him. But in February more tumors appeared in his chest, this time outside his ribcage. The cancer was spreading despite attempts to kill it. Piccolo endured more chemotherapy and a mastectomy in March to extract a tumor protruding from his chest. Doctors performed a follow-up operation in April to remove part of his lung cavity, then gave him a much stronger dose of radiation known as cobalt as a last-ditch attempt to thwart the cancer. He lost weight, and the cough, which had temporarily disappeared, returned.

Gale Sayers was closer to Brian Piccolo than he'd ever been before. He even donated his own blood to his stricken comrade. But Piccolo remained upbeat and would not allow his friend to feel sorry for him. Sayers knew Piccolo's chances of surviving weren't good.

Sports writers had voted Gale Sayers the most courageous man in the NFL for his comeback from knee surgery. When it came time for Sayers to receive the award, Brian Piccolo weighed heavily on his mind. He rose before hundreds of people that evening in late May in New York City and accepted the award, but on Piccolo's behalf. He shared with the audience these most memorable thoughts:

> *[Piccolo] has the heart of a giant and that rare form of courage that allows him to kid himself and his opponent—cancer. He has the mental attitude that makes me proud to have a friend who spells out the word "courage" twenty-four hours a day of his life. You flatter me by giving me this award, but I tell you I accept it for Brian Piccolo. It is mine tonight, it is Brian's tomorrow. I love Brian Piccolo, and I'd like you all to love him too. Tonight, when*

you hit your knees, please ask God to love him.

Most of the audience wept. Piccolo read about the speech at his Chicago home the next day. He greatly appreciated his friend's gesture of support and caring. But it was the joker in Piccolo who said to Sayers that day over the phone, "Magic, you're too much. If you were here now, I'd kiss you."

Brian Piccolo was readmitted to the hospital June 4 for more tests and chemotherapy. With his body weakening every minute and the cough causing him to convulse, Piccolo was but a pale reminder of what he once had been: strong, active, and full of life. Brian's parents and brothers arrived at the New York hospital on Friday, June 12, and were shocked to see him in such a fragile condition. His doctor advised his family that Brian's condition was grave.

On Monday, June 15, Brian felt distinctly better even though he was near death. Joy began to weep at his bedside, while Brian kept repeating the words, "I love you. I love you, honey. I love you. Please stop crying. We'll get out of here." She knew otherwise. Early in the morning on June 16, Brian Piccolo breathed his last breath.

Gale Sayers, as if out of empathy for Piccolo, had come down with a raging fever that same weekend and had been admitted to a Chicago hospital. His wife, Linda, called him with the news of Brian's death. So did McCaskey. Gale was heartbroken. The day of Brian's funeral, the words recited from scripture comforted him: "The virtuous man, though he dies before his time, will find rest." Joy also went out of her way to calm the sobbing Sayers. "Don't be sorry, Gale. I'm happy now because I know Brian is happy, and I don't have to watch him suffer any more. He's through suffering now." Gale Sayers was soothed by her words, but a piece of him had died along with Brian Piccolo, his good and compassionate friend.

We Are Not Alone

No man is an island, entire of itself; every man is a piece of the continent, a part of the main; if a clod be washed away by the sea, Europe is the less, as well as if a promontory were, as well as if a manor of thy friends or of thine own were; any man's death diminishes me, because I am involved in mankind; and therefore never send to know for whom the bell tolls; it tolls for thee.

—John Donne

Facts of the Matter
A Legacy of Compassion

After Brian Piccolo died, some of his friends, family, and football teammates in Chicago started the Brian Piccolo Cancer Research Fund. Over the years, the fund has raised millions of dollars for cancer research—research that has helped increase cure rates for certain types of cancer related to embryonal cell carcinoma, the type that killed Brian. The fund's present efforts are focused on seeking a cure for breast cancer.

Because of Brian's love for his wife's sister Carol, who has cerebral palsy, the Piccolo Fund also supports the work of the Clearbrook Center for the Developmentally Disabled, a facility in Chicago, where Carol lives and works.

To learn more about Brian Piccolo's legacy of compassion, visit www.brianpiccolofund.org/intro.html

DEDICATION

Roberto Clemente

Roberto Clemente was a hero in every sense of the word. On the professional baseball diamond as a Pittsburgh Pirate from 1956 to 1972, he frustrated opposing pitchers with his aggressive hitting. From his position in right field, he could peg a runner at any base with his strong, accurate throws. Off the field, he dedicated himself to improving the lives of others in his native Puerto Rico. He gave of himself and his money freely, and most of all, he loved people. Clemente's life and play paved the way for a new generation of Latino baseball players. His tragic and untimely death, in the service to others less fortunate, continues to inspire many.

➵-➴

Roberto Clemente Walker, known to the world as Roberto Clemente, was born August 18, 1934, in Carolina, Puerto Rico, in the heartland of the Caribbean island. He was the youngest of seven children born to Melchor and Luisa Walker de Clemente. His father earned forty-five cents a day, an above-average wage by Puerto Rican standards, working as a foreman in a sugarcane mill. His children enjoyed a happy, well-balanced childhood. Despite having little material wealth, the Clementes were rich spiritually. Faith in God formed the bedrock of their home. Roberto remembered his parents as "lovely persons" who taught him "the right way to live." He recalled, "I never heard any hate in my house. I never heard my mother say a bad word to my father, or my father to my mother."

At age eight, Roberto, a small boy with a contagious smile, played on his first baseball team—a group of neighborhood boys. His bat was a crudely formed tree limb, his glove a coffee sack, and the ball a collection of used rags. According to his father, "Roberto played surprisingly well against boys his age and older." His older brothers were sensational players who showed their shy younger brother how to hit and field. Roberto quickly fell in love with baseball. He often forgot to eat when a neighborhood game lasted past dinnertime.

In school, Roberto Clemente applied what he learned at home about loving and helping others. He organized his classmates to clean up the school grounds, and he impressed his teachers with his respectfulness. Even as a young boy he showed great compassion. When a neighbor died, he would run from house to house to spread the word and make sure people attended the funeral. He often volunteered to be a pallbearer in his community.

Young Clemente had one glaring physical attribute that set him apart. Even though he was a small boy, he possessed extremely large hands. As a former teacher explained, "Those big hands would express what he would not say in words." She spoke of the giving, caring qualities of his hands.

His hands also gave him a firm grip on a baseball and a bat.

A local baseball talent scout soon noticed Clemente's catching, throwing and batting skills. This scout had watched him play in many competitive softball tournaments and offered him a professional baseball contract with Santurce, a team that played in the Puerto Rican Winter Leagues. Though Clemente's father wanted a bigger contract than was offered his son, he soon agreed to the $400 bonus and $40 weekly salary. Although Clemente had succeeded in school and could have entered college, he joined the Santurce Crabbers on October 9, 1952. Like many rookies, he sat on the bench most of his first season and hit a meager .234. The next season, however, he got his wish for more playing time.

The Puerto Rican Winter Leagues attracted major leaguers from the United States who wanted to play ball year-round and stay sharp in the offseason. Some of the best and brightest stars in America descended upon Puerto Rico in the winter, giving local players the chance to team up with their American idols and showcase their own talents. In 1953 Clemente played alongside Willie Mays, the New York Giants star center fielder. He learned from Mays the "basket" catch, which he used the rest of his career. The tandem of Mays-Clemente wowed many fans that winter with their fielding and hitting. One of his teammates told him, "You'll be as good as Willie Mays some day."

Though American baseball "seemed so far away" to Clemente, nine different teams approached him that winter, eager to sign him to an American big league contract. The Giants were the first to call, but the Brooklyn Dodgers, afraid of the prospect of their archrival having both Mays and Clemente in the same outfield, bid a sizable $10,000 for him. Since Roberto was still underage, his father accepted and signed the Dodgers' offer. The Dodgers assigned him to their top minor league team in Montreal, the same farm team that Jackie Robinson played for before becoming the first African-American major leaguer in 1947.

Clemente's first season in professional baseball did not live up to his expectations. Montreal's manager, Max Macon, in an attempt to "hide" the young sensation from other teams, played Clemente only occasionally. Montreal did not want other big league teams to bid for his contract. When Clemente played well, which he did most of the time, Macon would remove him from the game. The few times he played poorly, he was kept in, thereby hoping to fool his would-be bidders. But the ploy did not work. Pittsburgh Pirates general manager Branch Rickey, who left the Dodgers in 1950 to work for the Pirates, picked Clemente up in the offseason for a mere $4,000. A confused Clemente recalled later: "I did not even know where Pittsburgh was." Although frustrated at being treated as mere property by owners, Clemente took consolation in the fact that he would get a chance to play in the majors, even though the Pirates were a desperately inept, last-place team.

Clemente's eager anticipation of his rookie season was overshadowed by his older brother Luis' diagnosis of brain cancer. To add to his misery, a drunk driver struck Clemente's car as he was returning home from the hospital after visiting his dying brother. He miraculously survived, but three vertebral disks were jarred out of place. From then on, he would suffer intense back pain that caused his characteristic habit of rotating his head and moving his neck side to side before every at-bat.

In 1950s America, Major League Baseball was peaking in popularity. The entry of Jackie Robinson into the majors in 1947 opened the way for other black players, and gradually white and black fans attended games together and rooted for their favorite players. Hispanic fans, however, had only a few players of Latino origin to cheer. When Clemente arrived at spring training in Florida, his reputation as a highly talented player preceded him. Yet the sports media quickly stereotyped him as they had other Latin American players. They branded him a "Puerto Rican hot dog," a label he resented because he said the writers did not even know him.

Worse than that, however, was the tendency of reporters to quote Clemente and other Latin players by writing their words phonetically. To quote Clemente by writing, "Me like hot weather, veree hot. I no run fast cold weather. No get warm, no play gut," made him sound unintelligent and invited racism and condescension. He even received his share of hate mail from anonymous people who said outrageous things such as "Go back to your jungle." But when he was told he could not dress for an exhibition game in Alabama in 1954, the problems of being dark-skinned in America became real. He had never even entertained the notion of being kept from doing his job just because of his skin color or ethnicity.

Sadness over his brother's untimely death and his own health hung over Clemente's head during his first season with Pittsburgh. His temper flared when he struck out, and he broke several dozen batting helmets that season, throwing them on the ground in disgust. Overall, though, his play stood out as a bright spot on an otherwise dismal team. In only his second major league game, against the New York Giants, Clemente hit a rare inside-the-park home run, and then later forced a double play at first base with a powerful throw. He had a flair for the dramatic in the field and when running the bases. With his hard-throwing, fast-running, solid-hitting, daredevil performances, he put on a show that Pittsburgh fans were not accustomed to seeing. This sensation from Puerto Rico gave them hope for the future.

Clemente soon became the sole reason many people attended Pirates games again. Each time he stepped up to the plate, the crowd rose to its feet and began cheering, even before he took his first practice swing. He loved to communicate with the fans at the stadium, often speaking to them in his Spanish or broken English from right field. They loved him back. Spanish-speaking fans would assemble in right field to root for their hero in his own tongue. People brought him sandwiches between doubleheader games. It did not hurt that he was extremely handsome. One associate at the time commented on how attractive he was to young women, with his striking good looks, broad shoulders, huge chest, and lean body. One writer noted, "He was without flaw physically." Despite his popularity, Clemente was still a rarity in the big leagues: a Latino ballplayer who was fast becoming a star in America.

No one worked harder than Clemente to help his team win. "A lot of people don't understand that you have to push yourself to play day after day," Clemente told his friend and American father figure, Phil Dorsey. But until 1960, his efforts went to a losing cause in Pittsburgh. In the preceding five years, Clemente's back, injured in the car crash back home, acted up and forced him to miss games due to debilitating pain. Again, the press roughed him up. "Hypochondriac" and "lazy" were terms they used in their articles to describe the ailing Clemente. They accused him of faking his injuries so he could rest. Yet Clemente cared deeply about the Pirates and would do anything to help them win.

In 1960, Pirates fans finally saw real results from the shot in the arm Clemente provided their team. They won the National League pennant and went on to meet the indomitable New York Yankees in the World

Series. The Series was tied at three games each, and in Game Seven the Pirates found themselves three runs behind. It was Clemente's infield single with two outs that extended their at-bat in the eighth inning, giving the following batter the chance to hit a grand slam home run. But the Pirates had to rally in the bottom of the ninth inning to beat the mighty Yankees on a home run by Bill Mazeroski.

No one was more jubilant than Clemente, who celebrated with Pittsburgh fans. After their World Series victory, he witnessed a mob of frenetic people outside the clubhouse: "It was something you cannot describe. I did not feel like a player at the time. I felt like one of those persons, and I walked the streets among them."

Now a recognized star, Clemente began to speak out about prejudices against Latino players. Baseball in Latin America did not suffer from segregation, as in the United States, and Latino players in the major leagues were baffled by such racism. "Latin American Negro ball players are treated today much like all Negroes were treated in baseball in the early days of the broken color barrier," Clemente said. Furthermore, "We [Latin Americans] bear the brunt of the sport's remaining racial prejudices." He emphasized the adjustment to American life that Latino players had to make before they could play their best baseball. Luis Mayoral, a Spanish-language sportscaster and close friend, believed that Clemente took the lead on this issue, even though other Latin players preceded him, because "he had the intestinal fortitude to become the spokesman for Latinos in the game. There have been other Latinos prior to him—great players, great individuals—but they did not have that makeup to really take the flag and lead Latinos in searching for recognition and respect in major league baseball." Many players feared management's retribution and felt inhibited by their own ability with the English language, and hesitated to speak out.

Roberto Clemente's concern for civil rights led him into a little-known relationship with Martin Luther King Jr. They met in 1964 on a farm Roberto owned in Puerto Rico. Luis Mayoral remembered: "Somewhere along the road in his major league career, he befriended Martin Luther King. I think that was a key relationship, in relation to the development of Roberto Clemente, the fighter for social equality." Later Clemente received a King medallion for playing in an All-Star game of blacks and Latinos to raise money for King's foundation. Clemente cherished that honor.

Clemente befriended other Latin American ballplayers, especially rookies like Panamanian catcher Manny Sanguillen. Sanguillen grew to love and respect Clemente as a friend, teammate, and as a Latino brother. He recalled in an interview, "When I joined the Pirates, he took me with him to best places, meet everybody. He did this all the time." Clemente, the star, helped him and other young players adjust to the language, the big league pressure, and the news media. He assured Sanguillen that even if he did make mistakes, it wouldn't be the end of the world. Clemente often took on the role of intermediary between the Latin American players for the Pirates and the team's administration.

The Pirates, in fact, were one of the most integrated teams in the National League. Black, white and Latino players mingled well both on the field and off. This was due, in part, to the leadership of Clemente, who consistently refused to make derogatory comments about any teammate. At a time in America when racial issues dominated the news and emotions ran high, the Pirates represented the possibility of races working together successfully.

In 1963, while in Puerto Rico, Roberto Clemente met a woman who captured his attention, Vera Zabala. Six months later, in 1964, they married. About 1,500 friends, family, and fans attended the wedding in Clemente's hometown in Puerto Rico. Within five years, they had three sons. Vera, according to a friend, was the only person who "knew what went on inside this complex man." Although a quiet woman who remained behind-the-scenes, she enhanced her new husband's life in ways that baseball could not.

Clemente's nagging injuries were tearing down his strong yet vulnerable body. Bone chips in his elbow, shoulder soreness, tonsillitis, a serious blood clot in a leg, malaria, and various pulled muscles and tendons were part of an array of injuries he incurred over the course of his career. The most hampering of all his injuries was still his chronic back pain. He sought relief from the team trainer, private chiropractors, and friends. At times, he would spend three hours before a game on the training table being rubbed down. After a while, he learned the technique for himself and offered to rub down his teammates who had similar pain. (He later opened a free clinic to treat people with ailing backs, and patients swore he had a healing power in his hands.)

In 1966, Clemente not only overcame potential career-ending injuries, he also had the season of a lifetime. He earned the Most Valuable Player Award in the National League, the first Latino player to win this highest honor. Rather than bask in his own glory, he reflected on the importance that this award had for others: "They [kids] will work harder, try harder, be better men." The veteran of more than a decade with the Pirates "got along with all his teammates" and had "great feelings for all the worries of the players" according to ballplayers who knew Clemente best. Even players from other teams consulted Clemente about their problems. "What am I doing wrong?" they would ask about their batting woes. Clemente never withheld advice and gave it cheerfully. One thing he insisted on, especially from his Latino friends, was that they maintain their pride in who they were as individual people worthy of respect. "You must never lose your dignity," he cautioned. To him, fellow Puerto Ricans were "somebody," regardless of their performance on a baseball field.

Clemente's value to the Pittsburgh club resulted in a record-breaking contract in 1967. He was the first Pirate in history to sign a one-year contract for six figures—$100,000. It took only minutes to reach the agreement, as had been the case with all of his previous negotiations. With his fame and fortune growing, Roberto needed to share himself, as well as his money. "He was always thinking of other people," said Phil Dorsey, with whom Clemente lived in Pittsburgh. Clemente turned his new-found celebrity into a mission, especially for kids. He spent much time with sick children at the Children's Hospital in Pittsburgh. His visits were often spontaneous.

While Clemente, according to Pirates manager Danny Murtaugh, was "the best all-around ballplayer I ever saw... without qualification," he never let the limelight set him apart from those he cared fervently about—namely his family, friends, and teammates. His greatest joy from success was "to erase the old opinion about Latins and blacks." A friend put it this way: "In a certain sense, Roberto was a man from another century... from a 'cultured' family in the sense of values." Another friend observed, "Money did not matter much to him." Not once did he hold out at contract time. He gave of his own money without reservation to those who needed it more than himself. "Baseball has enabled me to support eleven people and it has given me an education," he once said. He even gave a struggling forty-year-old pitcher who had finally made it to the majors half of his banquet fees. He often gave big tips to equipment managers and clubhouse men. It was not at all uncommon for him to hand out money to the poor children on the streets of Puerto Rico, or to anonymously provide for the needs of people with disabilities.

To Roberto Clemente, sports were an ideal way to teach kids "the values of good citizenship" and "that one must sacrifice a bit for the common good." He went to great lengths to ensure they had what they needed to excel both in sports and in life. He promoted responsibility and hard work and his belief that no man is create above another. He believed strongly in "giving everything I can according to my ability."

The years 1971 and 1972 were filled with bigger highs than Clemente had yet experienced in baseball. Many fans, now worldwide, saw in him the stardom of a Willie Mays or a Mickey Mantle, and put him in an elite group of the best to ever play the game. In 1971, he almost single-handedly won the World Series for the Pirates over the tough and favored Baltimore Orioles, even after losing the first two games.

Although he had been in the majors since 1955, Clemente was just beginning to get the national recognition others had received for lesser achievements. In 1971, he won the Babe Ruth Award as the World Series' outstanding player. Even many of his Oriole opponents admitted he was the best all-around player in either league. Then, by 1972, he approached a milestone: 3,000 major league hits. Only ten players in the history of the game had reached this mark. In the last game of the 1972 season against the New York Mets, as Pirates fans cheered in anxious anticipation, their hero hit a clean double and became the eleventh player ever to achieve that total. As Clemente rounded third, Willie Mays came over from the third-base dugout and hugged his rival, honoring him for such an outstanding accomplishment.

Because of nagging injuries, Roberto Clemente, now thirty-eight, had struggled to show his full potential. But baseball fans finally saw the flowering of his true greatness in 1972. "Now, at last, they know me for the player that I am," he said to a friend after that season—a season in which he had also won his twelfth consecutive Gold Glove award for fielding. But he had always enjoyed the respect and admiration of his countrymen and fellow Latinos. To them, he embodied success in baseball, the most popular sport in Puerto Rico, but he gave so much more in his tireless efforts off the field. Working constantly with youth in Puerto Rico, he wanted to "stop drugs before they start." He organized and coached kids and seeded the idea of a "Sports City," a large multi-sport facility in San Juan, with his own money. But his greatest humanitarian challenge lay ahead.

After spending the offseason enjoying his hobbies of sculpting, classical music, and writing poetry, Clemente took time to manage a team of Puerto Rican amateur All-Stars. In November 1972, he spent nearly a month in Nicaragua with them at the Amateur Baseball World Series. He made many friends there before returning to Puerto Rico for the holidays. Then two days before Christmas in 1972, the world woke to shocking news. A fierce earthquake had devastated Nicaragua's capital city, Managua. It was responsible for more than 25,000 deaths and took the homes of thousands more. When Roberto heard of the tragedy, he went into action as a citizen "ambassador," immediately appearing on television and organizing a relief effort—collecting food, clothing and money to send to his Nicaraguan brothers and sisters. Tens of thousands of dollars poured in as Puerto Rican people of all ages responded to his urgent plea. All Christmas Day, Clemente labored to box all donations while his own presents went unopened.

As Clemente worked around the clock, his friends and family worried about his health. "He forgot about eating," fretted one friend. Another attributed his intensity to a type of pride that did not allow discouragement. He planned to fly to Managua, but at first was dissuaded by friends from boarding the small, unstable cargo plane loaded down with supplies. But he then ignored their pleas after receiving an urgent request for sugar and medicine from his Nicaraguan friends, who told him that the government was commandeering the relief supplies that were arriving in the city. Clemente was outraged. He decided to deliver the next shipment personally, and invited his best friend, Manny Sanguillen, who was in Puerto Rico at the time playing winter ball, to come along. Sanguillen was eager to help but missed the plane after two bouts of car trouble delayed him.

Despite further warnings from friends, Roberto Clemente and three others pressed on. At five p.m. on December 31, 1972, he kissed his wife goodbye and boarded the aging DC-7 cargo plane headed for Managua. After several last-second delays, the plane finally taxied down the runway around nine p.m. and was in the air twenty minutes later. As it shook to reach takeoff altitude, the engines began to sputter. Less than one mile off the coast of San Juan, one engine caught fire. Three explosions followed before the plane crashed into the sea.

Officials informed Vera Clemente shortly after midnight on New Year's Day 1973 that the plane had crashed and that they feared there were no survivors. Clemente's devout mother clutched her Bible and read the Twenty-Third Psalm over and over again throughout the unbelievable night: "The Lord is my Shepherd, I shall not want... He leads me beside still waters, he restores my soul.... Even though I walk through the darkest valley, I fear no evil; for you are with me...." Word of the crash spread quickly across Puerto Rico, stunning the entire nation. Three days of national mourning were declared. For many years, Puerto Ricans would speak of that horrific New Year's in the same way Americans recall President Kennedy's assassination, remembering exactly where they were when they heard the news.

Many of Clemente's Pirate teammates were celebrating the New Year when they heard the news. Fans in Pittsburgh flooded the Pirate office with phone calls, just wanting to talk. Joe Brown, then general manager of the team, recalled, "That was devastating to me, not because I was general manager of the team, but more because of what he was.... He was loyal as could be, loyal to his family and his country, to his team, to baseball." Willie Stargell, another Pirates star player, with tears in his eyes as he summed up his feelings toward his friend: "Roberto was always trying to help someone.... He lost his life on the thirty-first of December, one of the most sacred days in Puerto Rico; it's a very religious day. It's when families traditionally are together. He broke that tradition because he felt the need to go to Nicaragua to help the victims of the earthquake. He gave his life trying to do something, at a very special time, when so many people tried to talk him out of going. But he had that determination."

Beyond Clemente's immediate family, perhaps no one took the news harder than Manny Sanguillen. For several days after the crash, Sanguillen stood with Vera Clemente and friends on Roberto's favorite beach to watch first a civilian team of deep-sea divers, and then a U.S. Navy team, search the turbulent 125-foot-deep waters while avoiding sharks. Only a few personal items of the victims were recovered. Sanguillen told Sports Illustrated later, "I was really hurt for his wife.... I know how much one and the other used to love, and be together. She went down to the beach every day too, to pray or see what she could do."

It was Sanguillen, though, who decided to do something to cope with his grief. He put on full scuba gear and made his own dives into the Atlantic in the vicinity of the crash. From a small boat, he could see the schools of sharks on the surface of the water, but he dove anyway, over and over, for several days from early morning until midnight. He even missed the memorial service a few days later. Yet he told the Sporting News, "So many things he help me. He go to my room, talk about every different hitter.... It was like my own brother die." Only one body, the pilot's, ever was found.

Bowie Kuhn, the commissioner of Major League Baseball at the time, said he did not know of any ballplayer he ever had more respect for than Clemente, a man who "had about him the touch of royalty." That respect was shared by so many others that a group of baseball writers arranged for Clemente to be inducted immediately into the Baseball Hall of Fame, waiving the usual five-year waiting period. On August 6, 1973, only seven months after Clemente's death, a ceremony was held in Cooperstown, NY. Kuhn spoke for many, in a voice broken with emotion: "So very great was he as a player, so very great was he as a leader, so very great was he as a humanitarian in the cause of his fellow men, so very great was he as an inspiration to the young and to all of us in baseball and throughout the world of sports.... Having said all those words, they are very inadequate to describe the real greatness of Roberto Walker Clemente."

The legacy Clemente left is indelible. His wife and sons carry on the work with Puerto Rican youth that he began. Latin Americans now comprise roughly twenty-five to thirty percent of all Major League Baseball players. One of baseball's biggest and most charismatic stars, Sammy Sosa, had declared Roberto Clemente his hero: "I wear his number [21], I watched his film, I studied his swing," says Sosa. Roberto Clemente's oldest son, Roberto Jr., told Sosa during the 1998 All-Star Game, "My father's spirit is with you." Roberto Clemente was the first Latin American to be immortalized in the Hall of Fame. But his claim to greatness far exceeds baseball statistics or any historic "first." A quarter of a century after his death, ex-commissioner Bowie Kuhn still had much to say about the legacy of the man. In 1998, he said that not only should Clemente be known as a great ballplayer, but one who wanted "to fulfill that obligation which players should feel to the people in the stands who adore them.... That is the legacy which I think he would have wanted to leave, a great professional who gave everything. Beyond that I'm sure he would want to leave the legacy that there is an obligation to be a role model.... He was a marvelous role model, not only as a player but also as a human being."

Much Is Required

For to those to whom much is given much is required. And when at some future date the high court of history sits in judgment on each of us, recording whether in our brief span of service we fulfilled our responsibilities to the state, our success or failure, in whatever office we hold, will be measured by the answers to four questions: First, were we truly men of courage.... Second, were we truly men of judgment.... Third, were we truly men of integrity.... Finally, were we truly men of dedication?

—President John F. Kennedy, Inaugural Address, 1961

Facts of the Matter
Honoring Dedication

I n 1972, Major League Baseball instituted the annual presentation of an award to recognize the player who "best exemplifies the game of baseball, sportsmanship, community involvement and the individual's contribution to his own team."

Originally known as The Commissioner's Award, it was renamed The Roberto Clemente Award in 1973 after Clemente's tragic and untimely death. The winner is selected from an annual list of thirty nominees, and is selected by a panel that includes the Commissioner of Baseball and Vera Clemente. The stellar list of winners, players who have demonstrated the value of helping others, includes Clemente's teammate Willie Stargell, as well as Kirby Puckett, Tony Gwynn, Al Leiter, Edgar Martinez, John Smoltz, and Carlos Delgado.

Delgado, the 2006 winner, is from Clemente's native Puerto Rico and has, throughout much of his career, worn Clemente's uniform number (21) to honor his countryman. Delgado's off-the-field work is focused on the importance of education. He sponsors two four-year college scholarships, and is the founder of Extra Bases, an organization with a mission "to help individuals and charitable groups in Puerto Rico and abroad who assist people in need." You can learn more about Extra Bases at www.extrabases.org.

HONESTY

Amos Alonzo Stagg

HONESTY: The quality or condition of being truthful; sincere.

In the late 1800s and early 1900s, the game of football was synonymous with brutality, injury and even death. Into that scene came Amos Alonzo Stagg, a great player and coach who brought a degree of civility to the sport. He saw football as a way to shape the lives of young men and instill in them discipline, courage and dedication. His coaching technique was tough and straightforward; he never used profanity, but he had his own strong, "clean" approach for motivating his teams. He inspired many players and fellow coaches with his decency and honesty. "Mr. Integrity," one of several nicknames by which Stagg was known, occasionally even refereed games in which his own team competed—opposing coaches knew him to be the most objective of referees even with his team on the field.

Amos Alonzo Stagg was born August 16, 1862 in West Orange, NJ, just outside New York City. The fifth of eight children born to Amos and Eunice Stagg, Amos Alonzo grew up at a time when the Civil War ravaged a divided nation and President Abraham Lincoln struggled to keep it together. Money was scarce in the Stagg home, and "Lonnie," as Amos Alonzo became known, helped his father as a cobbler, making and repairing shoes. Together, they also farmed their small plot of land to make a little extra money. The outdoor, physical work of threshing fields and baling hay appealed to Lonnie, who saw it as a way to strengthen his body and use his energy, which seemed boundless. Sports also gave him a physical and competitive outlet. Baseball and wrestling, which involved running, throwing, and muscular exertion, appealed most to Lonnie Stagg. In games with his friends, cutting corners or outright cheating was commonplace, but not for Stagg. He did not tolerate breaking the rules, loose as they were. His parents, both "humble and God-fearing," ingrained in him the concept of fairness, whether in sports or any other activity.

Lonnie Stagg showed leadership abilities as a growing young man. He often initiated athletic contests between his peers and even displayed a talent for inventing games. He, along with other boys he "coached," took the bladder of a hog, dried it, and blew it up to form an air-filled, semi-round ball. He then created a game, not all too different from football, which involved kicking, tossing and carrying the ball. Football, modeled after the British sport of rugby, was played at only a few private high schools and colleges in the late 1860s. This early version of the game resembled rugby in its ball-passing between players, field length, and objective to move the ball past an opponent's goal line. It also had the element of rough physical contact between opposing players.

The first intercollegiate football game was played in Stagg's home state of New Jersey in 1869. About fifty people attended this game between Princeton and Rutgers, which Rutgers won 6-4. But Stagg did not participate in organized football as a youth. The sport that most interested young Stagg was baseball, America's "national pastime." Stagg had a strong arm and played third base, a position tailor-made for his accurate throwing ability. When a professional league was formed in his hometown, Stagg and his friends watched the games though the knotholes in the surrounding fence, as they could not afford the gate fee of a nickel. The pitchers especially fascinated Stagg, and he began to practice pitching. He threw with greater speed than most boys his age or even older. After mastering the fastball, he worked hard to develop a curveball, the pitch that really seemed to baffle hitters. After weeks of practice, he finally figured out the proper technique. In addition to the fastball and curveball, he learned several other pitches, the combination of which made Stagg a "whiz kid" on the mound.

As much as Lonnie Stagg relished playing sports, he also knew the greater importance of education. His uneducated father helped instill in him a desire to learn, so schoolwork was a high priority for him. While most of Stagg's peers dropped out of school in their early teens to work for their families, Lonnie stuck with school. He attended Orange High School in nearby Orange, New Jersey. High school demanded many things of Stagg, including tuition payments, which made it necessary for him to hold several jobs in order to meet his financial obligation. But Stagg had learned from his parents the value of honest, strenuous, physical work, and he knew it would provide him the means to continue his education. He also viewed work as a form of sports training and discipline, which he applied to his baseball development.

Pitching for Orange High, as well as for a local Presbyterian church team, Lonnie impressed many fans and caught the attention of some collegiate talent scouts. He became a highly-prized college prospect in an era when recruitment of athletes was much less common than it is today. Stagg's high school principal recommended that he attend college, first because he saw Stagg's academic potential, but also because he exhibited a work ethic the principal knew would enable him to meet the rigorous demands of working, studying, and playing a sport. Stagg at first thought it a near impossibility for a poor cobbler's son to afford college, but advisers and friends convinced him otherwise. Instead of going straight to college, though, he spent a year at Phillips-Exeter Academy in New Hampshire in order to fulfill the academic requirements he would need to apply to his first choice, Yale University. At Yale, he could study divinity and achieve a goal he had set for himself, that of becoming an ordained minister.

Yale accepted a gleeful Lonnie Stagg, who turned down athletic scholarship offers from several other colleges. Yale also offered him a scholarship, but he turned it down, deciding that paying his own way by working would keep him honest, disciplined, and free of any kind of debt, financial or otherwise. He had dreams he hoped to fulfill at Yale, such as studying to become a Christian minister and playing baseball, but his conscience spoke loudly on the issue of not accepting scholarship money.

His Yale experience transformed Stagg into a scholar-athlete whose professors and coaches sought excellence in the classroom and on the playing fields. He knew he would try out for the baseball team because he had been recruited, but he initially showed little interest in playing other organized sports. At the urging of a friend and some football players, Stagg decided he would give football a try. He had seen one collegiate game, a Yale-Princeton contest, while attending Phillips-Exeter, and he enjoyed the action. Though the basic concept and physical challenges interested him, he never thought that he, at 5 feet, 6 inches tall and 150 pounds, could play this physically combative sport effectively. Like everything else in his life, though, he gave football everything he had to offer. His superior speed, strength and discipline made him an asset to the Yale "Bulldog" team.

The freshman Stagg showed promise from the outset, but the games in which he was given the opportunity to play were usually lopsided affairs with Yale trouncing its opponent. In a game that Yale won 75-0, the coaches let Stagg carry the ball as a running back. He proved to his coaches and fellow players that he could elude tacklers when running with the ball.

Though Stagg knew he had the raw ability to play football, he was limited to playing in just a few games his freshman year. Fall baseball practices conflicted with football and the baseball coach feared that Stagg might be injured on the gridiron, so he encouraged him to play baseball only. Stagg's decision to curtail his football activity showed the captain of the baseball team his devotion to the game. The captain, who decided the players' positions, initially assigned Stagg a spot at third base. Stagg quickly proved he could hit consistently, run fast, and throw with tremendous power. Though he was well-suited for third base, he badly wanted to pitch. His big break came when he relieved one of the regular starting pitchers. The captain observed Stagg's obvious genius on the mound and made him a full-time pitcher. During the spring season of Stagg's freshman year, he pitched in every game and led Yale to the Ivy League championship.

After the season, professional offers came rolling in, precipitating a bidding war for Stagg. One team, the New York Nationals, offered him an amazing fortune, $4,200, which he promptly turned down. "The whole tone of the game [professional] was smelly," said Stagg, referring to the poor character of the individuals (many gamblers, carousers, and underworld types) who typically played professional baseball. He instead rededicated himself as an amateur collegian and ultimately pitched Yale to five successive Ivy League championships (post-graduates were allowed to play). He was known as the nation's greatest collegiate pitcher at the time. Stagg had also begun to play football again, and by his senior year he made All-American as an end. Known as an extremely versatile athlete while he attended Yale, Stagg always placed the utmost priority on sportsmanship and abiding by the rules, playing the games in light of his desire to become a minister.

While Lonnie Stagg performed admirably and with brimming confidence on the athletic field, he recognized a particular character trait in himself off the field. In his role as a YMCA volunteer, he often became shy, even nervous, when speaking in public. A terrible stammer plagued him when he spoke before large audiences, and this embarrassment forced him to rethink becoming a minister, for public speaking was a large part of a minister's job. Though he did not waver in his deep desire to serve God in his career, he ultimately wanted a career that was the best match for his talents, abilities and vision for sports as a means of shaping the lives of young men. After many sleepless nights and much soul-searching, Stagg decided to withdraw from Yale Divinity School to pursue a career with the YMCA, an organization whose stated goal was to build a strong "mind, body and spirit" in the members of its community. The "Y" sought young men like Stagg to help field athletic teams of their own. It couldn't have been a better fit for Stagg, and his career crisis ended. He enrolled at the YMCA training school (YMCA International College) in Springfield, Massachusetts, in 1890, one of only four students in his class.

Within a short period of time, the YMCA recognized they had just the man they needed. Though football had been Stagg's secondary sport in college, the YMCA developed a team and tapped Stagg to be its coach. With only forty-two young men in the whole school, Stagg was not only forced to use every ounce of his ability as a coach to teach and train the few players on his team, but he had to play himself. His own peak physical condition provided an excellent example to the rest of the team. Necessity being the mother of invention, Stagg had to make the most of the limited talent he had to work with, and he achieved stunning results. In an ironic turn, Stagg, so well-known for his honesty, turned his attention to trickery, deception, and split-second timing to design plays that would fool the more talented opponents that his team would face. His innovative plays, utilizing split-back ends (who could run to daylight more easily) and the hidden ball play (completely legal under the rules at the time), drew notoriety from the press and contempt from his suckered opponents. *The Staggmen*, as his YMCA and future teams became known, even nearly defeated Stagg's alma mater, Yale, a national powerhouse. In two years, Stagg's teams won ten games in Springfield, causing one New York editorialist to write, "Mr. Stagg is without a doubt the finest football strategist in the United States." While in Springfield, Stagg also competed in the first-ever basketball game, a sport invented by one of his football players, James Naismith. He also coached the baseball team.

❖⋅❖

Football gained popularity in the late 1800s and early 1900s, but it also stirred up controversy. The action on the field centered on "mass momentum" plays such as the "V wedge," in which the largest blockers formed a "V" surrounding the ball carrier to pierce the opposition's defense. These plays brought massive (in both number and size) bodies together in tight formations and often resulted in bodies piled up three or four deep on the field. The scene was ugly, bloody mayhem. A memorable account of a game between Yale and one of its chief Ivy League rivals, Princeton, read: "Both teams got in some quite respectable slugging when they were sure the umpire was not looking and the man who did not have a bloody nose and mouth was considered a little out of fashion." Another account of the same game read, "In less than 15 minutes their jackets were soaked with blood. Some faces were decorated with gore and many looked as though a brick house had fallen on them." The direst recording of a college football game focused on a Yale vs. Harvard contest:

> *The football tournaments between the teams of Harvard and Yale recently had terrible results. It turned into an awful butchering. Of 22 people, seven were so severely injured that they had to be carried from the field in a dying condition. One player had his back broken, another lost an eye, a third lost a leg. Both teams appeared on the field with a crowd of ambulances, surgeons, and nurses. Many ladies fainted at the awful calls of the injured players.*

In 1905, eighteen football players died in the United States, and 159 more were seriously injured or maimed. Georgia outlawed the sport. Many called for a national moratorium on collegiate football. The sport engendered such brutality that parents of players feared for their sons' lives.

Despite its detractors, football was gaining fans. They admired the courage, the mental and physical conditioning, the strong spirit, and the will to win that the sport demanded. Proponents of football agreed, though, that the game needed to be revised, not abandoned. President Theodore Roosevelt, a strong supporter of the game, formed a national rules committee charged with the the task of reducing the game's brutality. Alonzo Stagg was appointed to this committee, and he proved instrumental in bringing sweeping reform to a sport he knew possessed more potential for good than harm. In addition to reforming the rules, Stagg, always an innovator, designed leg and hip pads to reduce injury.

In two short years at the YMCA, Stagg had earned himself a national reputation for training young men, as well as winning football games. In 1890 he accepted a new position at the University of Chicago as the chairman of their Department of Physical Culture and Athletics. Stagg's former Bible professor from Yale, Dr. William Rainey Harper, persuaded Stagg to join him in the developmental stages at the newly chartered university. Stagg respected Harper greatly and knew he would succeed in building a strong academic institution in Chicago. Harper convinced Stagg that, just as at Yale, athletics were to be a primary aspect of the schooling at the University of Chicago, and that Stagg was his man for the job of building the department from scratch. Stagg accepted the offer of $2,500 (only half what he could have made as a professional baseball player) and an associate professorship.

Lonnie Stagg had lofty goals for the athletic program he was designing. He wanted to field competitive teams, especially in football, but he did not care to compromise his firmly held belief that recruiting players was bad for sports and that fairness in play was as necessary a lesson to learn as any academic subject. "Money is damnation," said Stagg, who felt that doling it out to athletes sent them a mixed message. The subject most important to Stagg was the maturing of young men through training them in sports. His primary message for his players was that they were to work hard, play clean, and make personal sacrifices for the betterment of the team. Stagg was out "to produce the best that is in you, then [you] give freely and loyally to the team and university."

Early in his tenure at Chicago, Stagg devoted so much attention to his duties as head football coach that he neglected his own health. He nearly died of pneumonia, and a man of lesser physical stamina certainly would have. During his convalescence, he realized that he needed to be tougher and more disciplined with his players. He had suffered several losing seasons, and while doubting his own abilities as a coach, he knew that "genuine work" would produce good results. An innovation that he developed to help his team's chances was to install lights on the practice field so the team would not be limited by daylight practice hours. The work ethic he instilled in his players paid off in 1899 when Chicago won its first Western Conference championship (predecessor to the Big Ten).

His reputation as a coach, on the field and off, earned Stagg the nickname "Grand Old Man," which bespoke his old-fashioned values of honest effort, sportsmanship, and loyalty. "Winning is not worthwhile unless one has something finer and nobler behind it," said Stagg. Paul Stagg, the younger of Lonnie's sons, described his father well in an article titled "My Dad":

> *Although he had some fine teams and a good record as a coach; even though he made many contributions to the rules and to the play itself; even though he coached longer than any man coached and may ever coach, I believe perhaps his contribution to the game goes deeper. Perhaps it has been his steadfast belief in amateur sport, in football and in the youth of our nation. It may have been his forthright honesty and sense of fair play which once caused him in his early years of coaching to go out on the football field and object to a penalty on the opponent. It could have been his example of clean living and his expectation that his players would live up to the best standards.*

Alonzo Stagg was greatly respected by his players, who were motivated to obey Stagg's meticulous rules, such as no smoking, drinking and cussing, by the fear of disappointing their leader. "When I reach the soul of one of my boys with an idea, or an ideal, or a vision, then I think I have done my job as a coach." But Stagg had an unofficial partner on his coaching staff. His wife, Stella, whom he married in 1894, helped him with scouting reports, diagrammed plays on a chalkboard, and was her husband's most vocal fan during the games. Fittingly, the Staggs took their honeymoon to California to coincide with their football team's West Coast tour. The honeymoon never ended, neither in his marriage nor in his chosen profession—coaching. Lonnie and Stella had three children, two boys and a girl. His teams produced seven Western Conference championships and 268 wins (against 141 losses). What he gave to his players was far more than numbers could ever show.

Stagg was a man of vision. When the rules of football changed, created and implemented by a committee of which Stagg was a member, he designed plays to fit the more wide-open game. For example, when the forward pass was first allowed in the early 1900s, Stagg incorporated 64 pass plays in his playbook. Then, when other teams were just beginning to use passing in their offensive strategy, Stagg, along with his star quarterback, Wally Eckersall, perfected the spiral throw, which until then had not been developed. Passes were crude attempts to get the ball over the oppositions' heads, not the aerodynamic "strikes" that Stagg put into effect with remarkable precision. Stagg adapted the T-formation to better enable his new passing game, and it gradually became a collegiate standard, as did myriad other Stagg adaptations. The center snap, the huddle, the lateral pass, the man-in-motion, the place-kick, tackling dummies, and numbering plays and players, were all Stagg innovations.

The awarding of athletic letters was another Stagg invention. He awarded letters mainly on the basis of a player's "qualifying in manhood," not just on his ability as an athlete. Some of his better players did not earn letters, and he honestly confronted them with the truth when they hadn't shown the kind of spirit that he looked for in his lettermen, namely "faithfulness to practice and the rules of training, fidelity to fair play and good sportsmanship, loyalty to the athletic ideals of the university." Stagg refused to play favorites. His oldest son, Alonzo Jr., was an excellent backup quarterback. He failed to letter one year, not because of a poor attitude, but because his father withheld him from a game rather than risk the appearance of impropriety by putting him in for a reason other than that of injury to his starting quarterback. It left Alonzo Jr. just a few minutes shy of the playing experience necessary to earn his letter.

Stagg's tenure at the University of Chicago spanned forty-one years. A university policy forced him to retire at age seventy, much to his dismay. He still had the energy of a man half his age, even though he had coached a total of ninety-three seasons (forty-one football, thirty-two track, nineteen baseball, and one basketball) at Chicago. He also coached America's 400- and 800-meter athletes, and its 1,800-meter relay team, at the 1924 Olympic Games in Paris. He was a national treasure, but he did not quite feel like being put out to pasture in retirement. He accepted the position as head football coach at the oldest college in California, College of the Pacific, in Stockton. There, he brought fame, and amazing success, to a relatively unknown football program. In 1943, at the age of eighty-one and after a 7-2 season, Stagg was voted Coach of the Year. He retired a second time in 1946, only to join his son Alonzo Jr.'s coaching staff at Susquehanna University in southeastern Pennsylvania. Stagg assisted his son for five seasons and then returned to Stockton, California, to "officially" retire at age ninety.

In 1962, on Stagg's one-hundredth birthday, many around the country celebrated the life of a truly good man. But Stagg expressed a simple wish: "I would... like to be remembered as an honest man." He died in 1965 at the age of 103, a man whose simple honesty and goodness took center stage above all else. In a sport that offers glory, money and pride, Amos Alonzo Stagg's legacy remains in the valuable lessons he taught not only his players but the many who have played football since then. His lifelong message was pure and simple, yet it elevates sport to a higher level. "A real coach should try to impress upon them [players] the fine spirited values which come out of these sport games. The coach should be building integrity, honesty, and fair play for the community, the state, and the nation." His life and the lives of his players prove the worth of sports as a training ground for life. "The greatest satisfaction is to see youth develop," said Amos Alonzo Stagg, and he achieved that many times over.

Winning and Learning

No coach ever won a game by what he knows;
it's what his players have learned.

—Alonzo Stagg

Today's Character Builders

The name of Amos Alonzo Stagg may not be the most familiar to today's generation of sports fans, but his pioneering work in bringing honesty and true sportsmanship to participation in sports has led to the creation of organizations and resources that continue to achieve his goals. Citizenship Through Sports Alliance (www.sportsmanship.org) and Heart of a Champion (www.heartofachampion.org) are two such organizations that ensure the ongoing impact of Stagg's work long after his death in 1965.

The Citizenship Through Sports Alliance, or CTSA, is described as "the largest coalition of professional and amateur athletics organizations in the United States, focused on character in sport." From amateur and youth sport through professional leagues, CTSA "promotes fair play... to reinforce the value of sport as a test of character." With a number of initiatives in place to fulfill its goals, CTSA has worked with partners such as ESPN, USA Today, and The Gallup Organization to explore the challenges facing organized sports and character development.

Heart of a Champion believes that building character in America's young people and adults will improve "the quality of life in our communities." The organization's Heart of a Champion Character Development Program, directed at middle school-aged youth, uses stories from the world of sports as a key to promoting interest in character development. Heart of a Champion works with "schools, businesses, athletic associations, government at all levels, faith-based organizations, and community groups across the United States" to spread the word that character development is a necessary foundation for today's youth—who are tomorrow's leaders.

STRENGTH

Joan Benoit Samuelson
and Wilma Rudolph

Two Olympic runners in the second half of the twentieth century demonstrated how strength of body, mind and spirit can overcome limitations of many kinds. Joan Benoit Samuelson, a long distance phenomenon, and Wilma Rudolph, a lightning fast sprinter, showed their families, the world, and themselves just how far they could push themselves toward their goals when drawing upon all sources of strength.

※-※

All sports involve the expenditure of energy. Few sports, however, demand as much from its participants, both physically and mentally, as long distance running. Distance running presents a challenge to endure and to resist fatigue of monumental proportions. One of this sport's shining examples is Joan Benoit Samuelson. She is the embodiment of strength.

Joan Benoit Samuelson was born in 1957. She is a "downeasterner," having grown up in the state known best for its lobster harvest and rocky coastline: Maine. It's a place she has always loved and one that she credits for much of her success. She attributes the mental toughness that she has displayed over the years to having played sports under the adverse weather conditions typical of her home state in the fall and winter months. She trained so much in cold, windy, rainy and snowy weather that her desire to succeed as a distance runner had to be strong. Her determination served her well in competition. But just as important, it helped her rebound from several career-threatening injuries.

Growing up, Benoit Samuelson was a classic sportswoman. She

played many different sports and played most of them well. She was intensely interested in skiing, but a leg injury shortened what may have been a prodigious career. She played field hockey, a sport her mother had played in college, and was quite good. Of course, she enjoyed running, but she also liked sports traditionally reserved for boys, such as baseball and basketball, and played pick-up games whenever she could get the boys to let her. She grew up accustomed to competing against boys, especially her three older brothers who were also athletic. Although she was excluded from certain sports because of her gender, track and field gave her an early opportunity to join forces with her male counterparts. The added competition helped her work that much harder. She thrived in the midst of the most intense challenges: inclement weather, formidable opponents, and bodily injuries. Adversity seemed to propel her to greater achievement.

In a running career that spanned some twenty years, Benoit Samuelson kept a frenetic pace, letting little get in the way of improving her track skills. She admits in her book *Running Tide*, "I've had to face the fact that mine is an obsessive personality: sometimes my goals become more important than good sense. I keep pushing myself until I literally drop."

And drop was what she nearly did when she ran in a collegiate meet with a fever of 104. She did not know, nor did she *want* to know, that she had mononucleosis. She did not want to let down her teammates and coaches, so instead of dropping out of the race, she finished in a dizzying, feverish fog. To this day, she has finished every race she ever started, no matter how badly she has felt while running. "You call it pride," she writes, "but it's really fear—I'm afraid to relax my standards."

The greatest test of Benoit Samuelson's strength and ability to push herself came in the lead-up to the 1984 Summer Olympic Games. She sustained a knee injury during a twenty-mile run in South Portland, Maine and tried hard, by way of rest, medication, and shorter runs to avoid the inevitable surgery. Arthroscopic surgery was finally performed in April and an inflamed fibrous mass that was inhibiting movement was removed from her knee. Though the impediment had been removed, the question remained as to whether she could recover in time to not only run a marathon on May 12 at the Olympic Trials, but also to place in the top three so that she would qualify for the American team.

Recovery from the surgery required intensive therapy. For three weeks after the operation, she began her work at six o'clock in the morning and continued until midnight. She swam, biked, did exercises in a whirlpool, and ran short distances. In an amazing demonstration of strength and resilience, Benoit Samuelson went to Olympia, Washington, for the Olympic trials and won the marathon, which placed her on the U.S. Olympic team bound for Los Angeles and the 1984 Summer Games, at which the first Olympic women's marathon would be run.

She continued her recovery regimen over the course of the next three months and on August 5 a healthy Benoit Samuelson ran against the world's elite—Grete Waitz, Rosa Mota, and Ingrid Kristiansen—in the first-ever Olympic women's marathon. Once in the lead at the first water stop, Benoit Samuelson never relinquished her front position. The other runners waited for her to fall back, but she never gave them the chance to take the lead from her, relying on her physical and mental physical strength to propel her to the win. The victory, in which she defeated her closest competitor by a minute-and-a-half, was sweet satisfaction for someone who just a few months earlier had been considered unlikely to even make the United States team.

Joan Benoit Samuelson has given much and inspired many throughout her years of competition, but she's quick to credit others for her success: parents, coaches, and those pioneers in long distance women's racing. Such people include Bobbi Gibb, Katherine Switzer, and Mary Slaney, women who helped pave the way for that first Olympic women's marathon. The following year Benoit Samuelson won the prestigious Sullivan Award as the nation's most distinguished amateur athlete.

Joan Benoit Samuelson is a study in the mental attitude one must have to compete at the highest level in any sport. Intelligent, sensitive, and loving, she seems to have taken her international stardom in stride. She has never lost touch with her hometown roots and still prefers picking blueberries in her beloved Maine countryside to the hubbub that surrounds her athletic accomplishments.

❧

She can command a look of mingled graciousness and hauteur that suggests a duchess, but in a crowd that is one part Skeeter and 5,000 parts people, young men and babies will come to her in 30 seconds. —comments from Barbara Heilman about Wilma Rudolph, published in *Sports Illustrated*

Drive. Motivation. Heart. These are words closely associated with yearning and strength. Athletes are all driven to succeed, however they might define success. It's the ultimate goal that keeps one motivated. Life, though, being tenuous and unpredictable, often presents us with times when success seems to be but a dim vision, a mere speck on the horizon. Such is often the case when athletes are injured or suffer illness. Their recovery, if it occurs, is inspirational. Wilma Rudolph, the renowned track star and three-time Olympic gold medalist, is one of those sports heroes.

Wilma Rudolph was the twentieth of twenty-two children born to a Clarksville, Tennessee, family in 1940. Caring for so large a family, financially and otherwise, was an enormous challenge, especially when illness struck. A sickly child, Wilma had already experienced much adversity when at the age of four she was struck by polio, a disease that often results in paralysis. Wilma's parents never gave up hope when it came to their children, and they did everything humanly possible to prevent permanent muscular damage that might affect young Wilma's ability to walk. Frequent hospital visits that required lengthy driving time, hours of leg massages, and constant "fussing over" were all part of the treatment Wilma received from her parents and siblings. Despite such an intensive approach, there was still a distinct possibility that Wilma would never walk without the help of braces, and tremendous odds against her ever being able to run. Such possibilities did not deter the Rudolph family's determination to treat their ailing child.

Over the ensuing years, Wilma's leg condition gradually improved until one day, at the age of twelve, she no longer needed braces or special shoes to help her walk. From that point on, whenever she played and whatever she played, she played hard and fast. She excelled at basketball and track, using her strong leg muscles to jump high and run fast. Her high school basketball coach tagged her with the nickname "Skeeter." Coach Clinton Gray remarked, "You're just like a skeeter [mosquito]. You're little, you're fast and you always get in my way." The name stuck.

After playing basketball and running track in high school, in college Wilma was drawn to track by Tennessee State University's influential head track coach, Ed Temple. Tennessee State had a top-rated program, and Coach Temple offered Wilma a scholarship if she could make the sprint team called the Tigerbelles. After several attempts, Wilma ran a time that was fast enough to put her on the team and the scholarship was hers. It was no surprise to coach Temple, but Wilma's parents were elated. She would have a chance to get the education that they could not afford. Wilma's eyes were not just on running track, but on the educational opportunity she would be given. She made the most of both.

Wilma Rudolph's crowning achievement on the track came at the 1960 Rome Olympics, where she won gold medals in the 100-meter, 200-meter, and 4 x 100-meter relay. She won the Sullivan Award as the nation's outstanding amateur athlete in 1961, and became only the third woman member of the Black Athletes Hall of Fame in 1974. She met with several U.S. presidents, including John F. Kennedy, taught junior high school, and hosted television specials about Olympic athletes. Her primary focus in life, though, was her own four children.

Wilma Rudolph died of a brain tumor in November, 1994. Her greatest legacy is the Wilma Rudolph Foundation, which aims to provide young people with education and sports opportunities that will help them succeed in life. She worked diligently on this goal until her death and now many look at her as a true American hero.

Strive

Then welcome each rebuff
That turns earth's smoothness rough,
Each sting that bids nor sit nor stand, but go!
Be our joys three parts pain!
Strive, and hold cheap the strain;
Learn, nor account the pang; dare, never grudge the throe!
—Robert Browning

Facts of the Matter
The Eradication of Polio

P olio, the disease that Wilma Rudolph overcame, is a highly infectious disease that is caused by a virus. According to the Global Polio Eradication Initiative (GPEI), the polio virus "invades the nervous system, and can cause total paralysis in a matter of hours. It can strike at any age, but affects mainly children under three (over 50% of all cases). The virus enters the body through the mouth and multiplies in the intestine."

Though polio has no cure, a vaccine developed by Jonas Salk in 1955 has been very effective in reducing the number of cases, especially in developed countries such as the United States, where polio is now all but nonexistent. However, in 1988, at time when nearly 1,000 children per day in 125 countries were being paralyzed by polio, the World Health Assembly established the Global Polio Eradication Initiative (GPEI) in an effort to eradicate polio by the year 2000.

Despite the fact that its goal was not met, the GPEI has had great success. Since its inception, more than two billion children from countries all over the globe have been immunized. This effort required the cooperation of more than 200 countries and the help of 20 million volunteers. But its work is not done. To learn more about the fight to eradicate this disease, visit the GPEI's website at www.polioeradication.org.

HUMILITY

Eric Liddell

Scotland's athletic crown jewel in the 1920s was an Olympic sprinter named Eric Liddell. He was a man of deep religious convictions. By refusing to run a qualifying heat on a Sunday, because it was the Sabbath, Liddell sacrificed the opportunity to win an Olympic gold medal in his strongest event. Though this was by no means the greatest display of humility in Liddell's life, it is probably the best known. Chariots of Fire, a film about Liddell and his fellow Olympic runner Harold Abrahams, has been seen by millions and won the Academy Award for Best Picture in 1981.

❧·❧

Eric Henry Liddell's parents were Christian missionaries in Tientsin, China, where he was born in 1902. Eric was the second of four children. At the age of six he was sent to a London boarding school while his parents continued their work in China. He subsequently attended a Scottish boarding school, Eltham College, where in his early years he was described as "weedy" due to his lack of muscular development. By the age of fourteen, though, he had developed physically and began to excel at the rough sport of rugby. Young Liddell was best known for his speed and his ability to avoid tacklers. While at Eltham, he became captain of both the rugby and cricket teams. Even at this early age, he was a leader. His hard play was coupled with an unassuming style, inspiring his teammates to follow his example.

In 1920, Liddell enrolled at Edinburgh University in Scotland and began to run track. After an unimpressive beginning, his career took off at an event hosted by the Edinburgh University Athletic Club in 1921.

There he won the 100-meter sprint and was narrowly beaten in the 200-meter. The race winner, G. Innes Stewart, said of Liddell, "A new power in Scottish athletics has arrived." By 1923, Eric Liddell had broken several Scottish records in both events.

Though his track career continued its meteoric rise, a spot on the British Olympic team to compete in the 1924 Paris games was not a sure thing. Although he was well-known in Scotland, Liddell had yet to prove himself in England, especially London, which was not only the capital of the British Empire, but the nation's track and field capital. In July 1923, Liddell's performance at the AAA Championship in London made believers of any who questioned his Olympic potential. There he won both the 100- and 200-meter races against Great Britain's best sprinters. His time in the 100 meters, 9.7 seconds, was a British record. It would stand for thirty-five years.

His most shining moment leading up to the Olympics came a week later when he competed in the Triangular Contest between England and Ireland at Stoke-on-Trent, England. He won three events: the 100-, 200- and 400-meter races. But it was the way in which he won the 400 that clinched his spot on the Olympic team. Just into the first turn, Liddell was knocked off his feet and onto the infield. Initially thinking he might have been disqualified, he watched as several race officials motioned for him to continue. He scrambled to his feet and came from twenty yards behind to win the race. The newspaper *The Scotsman* reported the next day: "Veterans whose memories take them back thirty-five years, and in some cases longer, in the history of athletics, were unanimous in the opinion that Liddell's win in the quarter mile [400-meter] was the greatest track performance they had ever seen. He ran with his head cocked back and his arms beating the air." His unorthodox style of "attacking the air" would become his signature for the rest of his career. He later joked that this style came from his Scottish ancestors, who made raids into England and had to return quickly with all the booty.

To no one's great surprise, Eric Liddell made the 1924 British Olympic team in the 100- and 200-meter dashes, as well as the 4-x-100 and 4-x-400 relay teams. It was the highlight of an already stellar athletic career. Bound for the Paris Olympics in 1924, the twenty-two-year-old Liddell had a great chance of bringing back a gold medal in the prized 100-meter race. The first requirement in reaching his goal was to run well enough in the qualifying heats to get to the finals. Just weeks prior to the Olympic Games, the schedule of the heats was announced. Three of the four races in which he was entered had qualifying races on Sunday.

Because of this schedule, Eric Liddell declined to run. He took seriously the instruction of the Ten Commandments that one should honor the Sabbath and keep it holy. Without fanfare, he told team organizers that he would not compete in the 100-meter trials or the two relays. These powerful men, including the Prince of Wales—a man next in line to be king of England—pressured Liddell to make an exception. Newspapers called him a traitor to his country. But Liddell resisted the influence of both the British monarchy and popular outcry in order to follow what was, in his heart, a higher command.

Not long after Liddell's unpopular decision was announced, British Olympic officials offered him a spot in the 400-meter race. Although Liddell had not trained seriously for this event, he humbly accepted the offer and used the remaining few weeks to prepare for the longer distance. He was a long shot to win this event when the Olympics began in early July 1924. He would now compete only in the 200- and 400-meter races.

About 60,000 spectators were on hand for the Olympic opening ceremonies at the Stade Colombes, France's largest stadium. Forty countries were represented. The United States team had the fastest sprinters in the world, Jackson Scholz and Charles Paddock. With Liddell's choice to forgo the 100-meter sprint, British hopes for glory in the event were laid upon a Cambridge University student named Harold Abrahams. Abrahams had been Liddell's chief competitor in the 100-meters during the trials.

While Abrahams was qualifying for the 100-meter finals on Sunday, July 6, 1924, Eric Liddell was preaching a sermon at a church in Paris. Liddell felt burdened by the fact that he had disappointed his countrymen, but experienced an inner serenity as he preached. The next day, Liddell was in attendance to cheer for Abrahams in his quest for Olympic gold in the 100-meter final. In an amazing display of speed and technique, leaning forward dramatically at the finish, Abrahams became the first European to win the most coveted Olympic track and field prize. Liddell, ever the sportsman, cheered wildly along with his fellow countrymen. It would be his turn next, in the 200-meter event the next day.

In Tuesday's 200-meter qualifying heats, Liddell cruised through to the final along with Abrahams and four speedy Americans. Wednesday's final saw Americans Scholz and Paddock finish first and second in record time. Liddell finished third and Abrahams last. Liddell's bronze medal was met with little fanfare in the British press. The Olympic Games were only one of several international sporting events that were taking place at the same time, including the Wimbledon tennis tournament and the Henley Regatta, one of rowing's top races. Besides, it was only a bronze medal.

Not much was expected from Liddell in the 400-meter race. His fastest 400 was roughly two seconds slower than Great Britain's best runner in the event, Guy Butler. But because of Liddell's controversial decision not to run in his strongest race on Sunday, all eyes were fixed on him as he prepared to run the 400-meter qualifying heats on Thursday. He would compete against the world's best 400-meter specialists, including the world record holder, American Horatio Fitch.

Eric Liddell succeeded in the qualifying heats and progressed to the finals, which took place on Friday. He outran all his opponents in what was literally a runaway victory. His victory shocked the crowd and delighted his countrymen. They cheered exultantly. In his gold-medal effort he won the race by five meters and set a world record of 49.5 seconds. Spectators, coaches, and other athletes were amazed that a runner with "defects of style" such as running with his head back and flailing arms, could win so decisively. Liddell did not linger long in glory at the stadium after his gold medal victory, though—he had a sermon to prepare for Sunday.

British newspapers did not hesitate to praise his efforts. On Saturday, July 12, the *London Times* reported: "E. H. Liddell today won the Quarter-Mile (400 metres) for Great Britain in what was probably the most dramatic race ever seen on a running track." Further they exclaimed, "So, in one wild minute, what had been the dullest of days was turned into about the most memorable that the Olympic Games have ever seen." Liddell's 400-meter victory was "the greatest achievement in the [1924] Olympic Games so far... the crowning distinction in Liddell's great career on the track, and no more modest or unaffected world champion could be desired," reported Scotland's *Bulletin* newspaper.

Liddell took such praise in stride.

Liddell soon graduated from Edinburgh University, only a month after his stunning victory. University officials made elaborate preparations for the ceremony to honor their world-famous student. They prepared a crown of wild olive and placed it on Liddell's head in a ceremony reminiscent of the Olympics of ancient Greece. The other students burst into "He's Jolly Good Fellow" and paraded Liddell on their shoulders through the streets to the church where the rest of the graduation was to take place.

Later, after a luncheon, his classmates persuaded him to make a speech. A hush fell over the crowd as Liddell told them, in his quiet and deliberate manner, of his plans to perform evangelistic work with Scottish boys and then go to China as a missionary. He inspired his classmates and was praised in the Edinburgh University magazine. "Success in athletics sufficient to turn the head of any ordinary man, has left Liddell absolutely unspoilt, and his modesty is entirely genuine and unaffected.... What he thought it right to do, that he has done...yielding not one jot or tittle or principle either to court applause or to placate criticism.... Devoted to his principles he is without a touch of Pharisaism." With these words, the university magazine recognized the humility with which Eric lived out his religious convictions.

Eric Liddell became a Scottish national hero. He spent the rest of 1924 and much of 1925 studying divinity in Scotland and speaking to packed audiences all around the country as part of the Glasgow Students Evangelistic Union. These meetings were called "Manhood Campaigns," and one newspaper summarized their message as, "Playing the game of life in a manly and Christian way" (though today we might substitute the word *mature* for *manly*). By speaking to audiences, Eric Liddell was using his gift of communication to reach people of diverse backgrounds. He had the unique ability to engage strangers as friends, making them feel important and challenged at the same time.

In 1925, less than a year after his rise to fame, a calling to mission work led him overseas to become a teacher and coach in an Anglo-Chinese college. He left the notoriety he had attained in Scotland and returned to the land his parents had served so faithfully. He did so despite warnings that internal political strife in China made working there extremely dangerous. Eric's father sent his son the following report just prior to Eric's arrival in China that summer:

> *This year we have had the triple evils of war, flood, and famine. Any one of these is bad enough, but all three together have made for suffering that is very hard to realize. Ruin has overtaken great numbers of families, and it will never be known how many lives have been lost, through these visitations. Oh, the horror of it all!*

His father also told Eric of China's dangerous and dramatic political uncertainties. "A nation is in travail," Eric's father wrote, and it was to an unsettled nation that Eric Liddell returned in 1925. Upheaval had marked the beginning of the century in China, with the Boxer Rebellion of 1900. In this peasant uprising, there were severe reprisals against foreigners, and missionaries were easy targets. By the time of Eric's return, two factions vied for power in China—the Nationalists and the Communists. And Japan waited for its opportunity in the wings. The Liddells were undaunted in their educational and ministerial efforts to the Chinese people, so the warnings by Mr. Liddell had scant effect on Eric. He immediately poured himself into teaching science to the villagers. Though he did not have a commanding presence in the classroom, Liddell's love for the students helped him enjoy his job. He loved seeing those in his charge laugh, and he skillfully related with them as fellow human beings. He also coached them in sports, and the students began breaking school track and field records.

Just prior to his first furlough and return home in 1930, Eric Liddell announced to his friends that he was getting engaged to be married to a long-time family friend, Florence McKenzie, whose parents were Canadian missionaries in China. The engagement lasted almost four years as Florence finished her nurse training in Canada. In 1934, on the mission field in Tientsin, China, Eric's birthplace, he and Miss McKenzie were married. The Liddells and McKenzies were quite well-known and popular with the Chinese, so the wedding was front-page news in the *Tientsin and Peking Times* and the *North China News*.

Within the first three years of their marriage they had two daughters, Patricia and Heather. Eric adored his children, but the demands on his time as a missionary meant he saw little of his own family. In 1937 he made a prayerful decision to concentrate his missionary efforts in a remote province known as Siaochang. There he joined his brother, Rob, who was a doctor, and they worked together in an area that was devastated by war and drought. Their mission was grossly understaffed, which made visits home difficult and uncommon. Once again, Eric Liddell had left the comforts of home behind, compelled to serve those in greater need. The political climate was tumultuous, as now the Japanese had invaded northern China. This time, his work would put him in the midst of upheaval, war and suffering.

The Sino-Japanese War intensified and the Siaochang Mission became the outpost and hospital for many refugees and wounded soldiers from four different armies. In 1943, the war finally engulfed the mission, and all the missionaries were interned in a Japanese prison camp at Weishein. Death, starvation and despair characterized life in the camp. Shortages of food and terrible heat added to the misery. Eric Liddell made it his goal to alleviate the suffering of his fellow prisoners. He organized classes, coached athletic games, and did what he could to treat them medically. However, his own health had failed, most likely as a result of fatigue and malnutrition. Most did not know the extent of his illness, because he made it his business to help others.

Eric Liddell suffered a massive brain hemorrhage and died at the Weishein Prison Camp in 1945. He was forty-three years old. His death as a prisoner of war did not go unnoticed. It had been twenty-one years since his stunning gold-medal victory at the Paris Olympics, but he still was remembered with great honor. *The Glasgow Evening News* declared, "Scotland has lost a son who did her proud every hour of his life." Sports writer A. A. Thompson eulogized Liddell by writing: "During the worst period of his imprisonment he was, through his courage and cheerfulness, a tower of strength and sanity to his fellow prisoners. To many sufferers he brought the only comfort that captivity allowed. It is one of the deep sadnesses of life, that while so many survived the years of captivity, E. H. Liddell, who had helped so many, did not. He was one of the most chivalrous of Scots, as an athlete and as a man."

Thousands attended memorial services for Eric Liddell in many parts of Scotland and Canada. Many friends and associates paid tribute to the unassuming hero on a February day in 1945. One of them, the manager of the Rangers Football Club in Scotland where Eric Liddell would draw huge crowds, remembered him:

> *He deliberately sacrificed a fine chance of one Olympic title because of his religious convictions. He just as certainly put aside a career of brilliance and affluence to serve his master in the most practical of all forms of Christianity.... Sport gave to Eric Liddell its highest honours; nevertheless, it is true to say that he honored sport rather than sport honoring him....*
>
> *In these days of exaggerated hero-worship and publicity for sports champions, Eric Liddell's example reminds us to put*

things in their proper perspective. Sport to him was sport—not the be-all and end-all—and success in it did not prevent him from picking out the things spiritual from the things temporal.

Eric Liddell shared himself through athletics, inspiring others by his rare ability and his humbly held convictions. As a young man, in the spotlight of Olympic gold, he did his best and received the whole world's honor. As a seasoned servant, he died in the dust of a Japanese prison camp, having done his best. The imperishable crown of victory clearly adorned Eric Liddell.

In 1980, the United States boycotted the Olympics held in Moscow. A Scotsman named Allan Wells won the 100-meter race, the most coveted title in track. Fifty-six years after the 1924 Olympics and Liddell's refusal to run that same race, his influence still was felt. When Wells was asked if he had run with Harold Abrahams, the 1924 gold-medalist, in mind, he replied, "No, this one was for Eric Liddell."

Three Ideals

I have three personal ideals. One, to do the day's work well and not to bother about tomorrow.... The second ideal has been to act the Golden Rule, as far as in me lay, toward my professional brethren and toward the patients committed to my care. And the third has been to cultivate such a measure of equanimity as would enable me to bear success with humility, the affection of my friends without pride, and to be ready when the day of sorrow and grief came to meet it with the courage befitting a man.

—Sir William Osler

Facts of the Matter
Humility in All Walks of Life

The importance of humility is not only recognized in the contexts of sports and religion. The philanthropist John Templeton established a foundation that would empower people in many walks of life—the natural and human sciences, philosophy and theology, and education, to name a few—to explore the big questions that life poses. "These questions," the Foundation's mission statement explains, "range from explorations into the laws of nature and the universe to questions on the nature of love, gratitude, forgiveness, and creativity."

The Templeton Foundation has established "core themes" that describe its interests and guide it in choosing among the projects that seek funding from the Foundation. One of these themes is humility:

> *The theme of humility has been a core aspect of John Templeton's philanthropic vision since he established his Foundation. Indeed, the motto of his Foundation ("How little we know, how eager to learn") helps to define our Foundation's "Humble Approach Initiative."*

To this end, the Templeton Foundation has supported a study of the virtue of humility in psychology and it continues to look for proposals that examine humility's role in other areas, such as science, philosophy and theology. It is the Foundation's hope that humility and open-minded inquiry will lead to breakthroughs and discoveries that will advance the progress of the human race. Learn more about The Templeton Foundation at www.templeton.org.

INTEGRITY

Arthur Ashe

INTEGRITY: The quality of being of sound moral principle, of acting upon knowledge of right and wrong.

A native of Richmond, Virginia, Arthur Ashe embodied grace and gentility in tennis, whether he was playing the game on the court or representing it off the court. His parents, strong and independent-minded people, laid a firm foundation of personal and familial honor while raising Arthur and his younger brother, Johnny, in the racially segregated South. The vast economic and social divide between blacks and whites in the 1940s did not deter the Ashe family from teaching their children values such as honesty and integrity. Mattie, Arthur's mother, kept education and spiritual reverence high above all other priorities in raising her sons. Ashe, the first African-American male to star in tennis (in the 1960s and 1970s), was a credit to his city, his family, his nation, and the world. He led by example, responding to personal and racial insults with a calmness that belied his inner determination to change the tone of race relations in America and throughout the world.

◈

Arthur Robert Ashe Jr. was born July 10, 1943, in Richmond, Virginia. The mainly black hospital in which he was born reflected the prevailing attitude of keeping whites and blacks separate, even in large public institutions. His father, Arthur Ashe Sr., worked as a handyman (carpentry, painting, gardening, etc.), and often held down several jobs at one time. When Arthur Jr. was six years old, his father took a job as the director of a Richmond city park, Brook Field, and the Ashe family moved to a home provided for them on the park grounds. The park offered, besides natural beauty, the opportunity for young Arthur to play tennis on any of its four tennis courts, which he did often. He enjoyed other sports, such as baseball, but he displayed a greater natural ability on the tennis court.

Although Arthur's parents approved of and encouraged the athletic diversion that tennis provided, they made sure that his education came first. Their discipline helped keep Arthur on track. Arthur read prolifically and studied diligently in school. Mattie's protective love for her son and doting nature endeared her to him. She often played music for him, and they read the Bible together. Arthur grew extremely close to his mother.

Arthur's brother, Johnny, was born in 1948. Tragedy struck the Ashe family in March 1950, however, when Mattie took ill during her third pregnancy. She never recovered and died shortly after entering the hospital with toxemia, a dangerous condition that causes high blood pressure in pregnant women. Mr. Ashe and Arthur Jr., then six years old, took Mattie's death hard. So difficult was his mother's death that Arthur refused to go the funeral because he did not want to see her without the abundant life she always exuded. She had been his emotional anchor and spiritual bedrock. Her departure left a serious void in Arthur's life.

Mr. Ashe sought the assistance of a friend, an elderly widow named Mrs. Otis Berry, who graciously agreed to help raise the two Ashe boys. Mr. Ashe became even tougher as a disciplinarian, knowing that without their mother his sons would need extra guidance from him. He eventually remarried in 1954, but Arthur never became close to his stepmother.

Brook Field provided recreation for many athletic African-Americans in Richmond. Ronald Charity, a student at nearby Virginia Union University and one of the nation's top African-American tennis players, played often on the Brook Field courts, enough that Mr. Ashe hired him as a summer tennis instructor. Charity noticed the skills and talent of his boss' son and set about to develop the potential he saw in Arthur Jr. As his early coach, Charity worked hard to change the attitude that Arthur had started to develop by being one of the better players in the area. "I bawled him out for it [bad attitude] and told him if he continued to do anything like that, I wasn't going to be bothered with him anymore." Ashe's court behavior improved immediately, and with Mr. Ashe's reinforcement, Arthur's attitude became one of the strongest dimensions of his game.

Ronald Charity took Arthur under his wing and in 1953 introduced Arthur to his tennis mentor, Dr. Robert Walter Johnson. Johnson, a renowned tennis player and coach, lived in nearby Lynchburg, Virginia. That summer was a time for learning the game of tennis and the shot-making, strategy and thinking that would be necessary to play at a higher level. Arthur, ever the student, soaked up the lessons.

From 1953 to 1960, Arthur Ashe spent summers training with Dr. Johnson and traveling the east coast playing in tournaments. Ashe said of this experience, "I was schooled in the strictest manners and taught an unshakable oriental calm." Dr. Johnson taught his players how to keep their cool during a match, especially when playing against a white player. He wanted his players to avoid racial confrontations and concentrate on the game itself, even when the white player might get the benefit of generous calls from the officials. Such cheating was a fact of life for a black tennis player in a predominately white sport.

Another fact of life for Arthur and other black players was that of being excluded from major youth tournaments on the basis of race. One of the first such episodes occurred in his home city. Although he was by far the best player in the area, ranked fifth in the nation in the junior division of the United States Lawn Tennis Association (USLTA), the tournament directors decided not to accept his application to play in the mid-Atlantic regional in Richmond. Their decision was based largely on the fact that the host clubs in Richmond had a strict whites-only policy, with no exceptions for a young, talented African-American player. "The inequities imposed by racism were frustrating," Ashe would later write, "but I was fortunate to be surrounded by a devoted father and other black people determined to push me along, broaden my horizons, and help me develop a sense of myself that ignored the limits white Richmond wanted to impose at the time."

Arthur did not let the roadblocks in his native city deter him from playing the game he loved and competing in other national tournaments. Dr. Johnson made sure that Arthur's talent was showcased wherever possible, and in November 1960, Ashe became the first black male to win a major USLTA event. Shortly thereafter, the coach of one of the top collegiate programs in the country, UCLA, called and offered Arthur a full scholarship, the first offered to a black tennis player in the school's history. The national ranking of UCLA's program, and the strong reputation of its coach, J. D. Morgan, helped Ashe decide quickly that he was bound for the west coast to further his education and continue his tennis ascent.

"When I decided to leave Richmond," said Ashe, "I left all that Richmond stood for at the time—its segregation, its conservatism, its parochial thinking, its lack of opportunity for talented black people. I had no intention then of coming back." The impressionable boy of the 1950s became a resolute young man who had a mission to accomplish—a mission that included tennis, but was not exclusively focused on the sport. His conscience had been seared by racial inequality and injustice, not just from what he experienced firsthand in Richmond, but by what he observed taking place all over the country. Arthur, at the direction of Dr. Johnson and then J. D. Morgan at UCLA, decided to let his actions on the tennis court do his talking. His initial "protests" took the form of quietly shattering the stereotype that whites had of blacks. He caught the nation's attention as an outstanding tennis player as he rose during his freshman year of college to become one of the top thirty amateurs and a member of the Junior Davis Cup squad.

Ashe stayed busy at UCLA. As part of his scholarship requirements, he had to perform 250 hours of on-campus work, and he also had an ROTC (officer's training) military commitment to fulfill. Coach Morgan helped Ashe juggle his activities as Arthur continued his rise to prominence in tennis. Though he began his career at UCLA ranked third on the team, he had trouble concentrating on his game and often looked as if he were not playing his hardest. Still, he finished his first season undefeated.

Friendships with teammates and with a Los Angeles tennis professional highlighted Ashe's first two years at UCLA. One of his teammates, Charlie Pasarell, the top player on the team, boycotted a tournament in a show of support for Ashe when the host club excluded him because of race. His childhood tennis idol, Pancho Gonzales, was the club professional at the Beverly Hills Tennis Club, and he befriended Ashe.

They even became practice partners, and Gonzales, a highly successful professional, gave Ashe the benefit of his experience and knowledge. Gonzales helped Ashe refine his strokes and gave him strategic pointers. Ashe's game took a leap forward in 1963 during his sophomore year at UCLA when he qualified for Wimbledon, and then in 1965 when he won the NCAA men's singles championship. It wasn't long before Ashe was a regular on the world stage, qualifying for all four major tennis events: the Australian Open, the French Open, Wimbledon, and the U.S. Open. His game had a star quality, and it proved only a matter of time before he was beating the best players in the world.

Arthur Ashe won many awards during his tennis career, including the U.S. Open in 1968, the Australian Open in 1970, and Wimbledon in 1975. His prized possession, however, had nothing to do with the glory and fame he achieved on the tennis court. He begins his memoir, *Days of Grace*, by saying: "If one's reputation is a possession, then of all my possessions, my reputation means the most to me. Nothing comes even close to it in importance." To illustrate his point, Ashe describes a point in a match against Stan Smith. The ball had landed close to the line. Smith had the best view, and Ashe accepted Smith's call:

> *I have tried to live so that people would trust my character, as I had trusted Stan Smith's. Sometimes I think it is almost a weakness in me, but I want to be seen as fair, honest, trustworthy, kind, calm, and polite. I want no stain on my character, no blemish on my reputation.*

Ashe was a champion in every sense of the word. As a player, he scored great victories all around the globe. As a human being, he was an even greater champion. In his personal life, he was a devoted husband and father. In the public realm, he supported causes that helped bridge the racial divide He circled the globe as the U.S. Davis Cup captain from 1980 to 1985, winning the Cup in 1981 and 1982. In the process, Arthur Ashe became a diplomat for the cause of racial equality. He fought against circumstances and issues that threatened the fabric of society. For example, he began protesting South Africa's policy of racial segregation and inequality, known as apartheid, in 1970. He backed his philosophy with actions, using his athletic status and international profile as a tool in the struggle against injustice. Nelson Mandela, South Africa's most prominent black leader, was imprisoned for twenty-seven years under the apartheid system. Mandela respected Ashe so much that upon his eventual release from prison he wanted to see Ashe as soon as possible.

◆·◆

It is perhaps a strange irony that with all the heart and energy with which Ashe approached his tennis game and life, he suffered a heart attack in 1979. He underwent heart bypass surgery twice, in 1979 and

1983. In 1992, a national newspaper revealed that Ashe had the human immunodeficiency virus (HIV). Ashe and his wife, Jeanne, had known this and kept it secret since 1988. They had wanted it to remain secret until after his death, but with the public revelation of his condition, Ashe prepared to approach his illness with the same integrity and intensity with which he had overcome all the challenges in his life. In the 1980s, the blood supply for life-saving transfusions needed major surgeries was not always pure, and Ashe contracted HIV during one of his two heart surgeries.

True to form, in the time he had left to live Ashe devoted much of his life to educating the public about AIDS and raising money for much-needed research. With the energy of a tornado, he spent countless hours writing or speaking on this subject that was simultaneously so personal and so public. He gave of himself to the very end, first and foremost to his wife and daughter, but also to the causes that meant so much to him. Arthur Ashe was triumphant even in death: Even though he had every reason in the world to feel embittered by the injustices of racial prejudice and the horrible illness that ultimately took his life, he had the attitude of a winner and spirit that kept him focused on higher principles.

Ashe died from complications due to AIDS on February 6, 1993, a true champion and a man whose character and integrity will endure far beyond his years. In 1996 a statue of Arthur Ashe was dedicated on Monument Avenue in Richmond, Virginia, Ashe's hometown. For more than a hundred years Monument Avenue had honored Confederate war heroes such as Robert E. Lee and Thomas "Stonewall" Jackson. It took city leaders years to decide where to place Ashe's statue, with many protests against placing it where it now stands. As uniformed Confederate heritage protestors stood in the background waving confederate flags, speakers and dignitaries addressed the audience to share their thoughts about Arthur Ashe and to put the day into proper perspective. Even in death, Ashe continues to challenge and break down racial barriers.

One speaker, an African-American woman who knew Arthur as a child, said, "This is the proudest moment of my life. I finally feel like I can walk along Monument Avenue with my head held high, and that I belong here."

Clothed with Integrity

If everyone were clothed with integrity, if every heart were just, frank, kindly, the other virtues would be well-nigh useless, since their chief purpose is to make us bear with patience the injustice of our fellows.

—Molière

Facts of the Matter
Ongoing Help for Urban Health

Arthur Ashe was a forward thinker who never forgot, even in the face of his own struggles, that he had the power to improve the lives of others. In his autobiography he wrote, "The absence of coherent national health care policy is, in my opinion, one of the major disgraces of American life. Greed should not blind doctors to the devastating effect of the absence of such a policy on the American poor and middle class." Two months before his death, Ashe made a final, lasting effort to address healthcare in the United States by establishing the Arthur Ashe Institute for Urban Health (AAIUH).

Headquartered in Brooklyn, New York, and focused on the city's five boroughs, the Institute develops programs that encourage people to take care of their health in a proactive way. AAIUH takes its programs to the city streets—beauty salons, laundromats, libraries, houses of worship—and partners with government and private organizations to promote healthy living habits to improve access to healthcare. Tennis stars Venus Williams and Andy Roddick, retired baseball player and announcer Keith Hernandez, and writer Maya Angelou are among the individuals who have given of their time and resources to make life better for New Yorkers who face health challenges. The Institute's strategy includes finding ways to replicate the programs they develop in other parts of the country.

More information about AAIUH can be found at the Institute's website: www.arthurasheinstitute.org.

NOBILITY

Branch Rickey and Jackie Robinson

No greater act of nobility can rival that of one person putting him- or herself at risk for the sake of another. Such nobility is seen in Branch Rickey, the Brooklyn Dodgers general manager, and Jackie Robinson, the star Dodger player, and is exemplified in the actions they took and the manner in which they carried themselves in 1947. That was the year that these men shocked the world by breaking Major League Baseball's color barrier.

❧❧

The end of World War II in 1945 saw a post-war euphoria throughout the United States as it rose to the level of world super power. Part of this rise included encouraging healing and reconstruction in Europe, even as racial divisiveness raged in America. The signs of separation were everywhere, from the military to the country's beloved pastime, baseball. At that time, there were two distinct leagues: the entirely white major leagues and the all-black Negro League. This segregation dated back at least as far as the 1890s, when white baseball executives established an unwritten rule barring blacks from the major leagues. The exclusion of black players had nothing to do with talent. It had everything to do with a handful of powerful men whose racial prejudices and fears kept them from dealing fairly with black players. With this backdrop, Branch Rickey, general manager of the Brooklyn Dodgers, and Jackie Robinson, an outstanding Negro League ballplayer, met in 1945.

Wesley Branch Rickey was born in 1881 to an Ohio farming family of modest income and strong Protestant religious beliefs. Although Branch and his brother played football and baseball every day, Sunday was reserved for church and rest. Playing games such as baseball and football became primary entertainment for the active Rickey boys, and one could find them tossing a ball any day of the week, except Sunday. As a youngster, Branch promised his mother that he always would observe the Sabbath.

After earning the equivalent of a high school diploma, Rickey was accepted at Ohio Wesleyan University. He worked doggedly on his studies to compensate for the lack of preparation and held down many different jobs to pay his tuition. Despite this schedule, he still made time for athletics, which provided an outlet for his vast energies. At the time, collegians such as Rickey were allowed to play in football and baseball semi-professional leagues for pay. Almost more than the actual game, Rickey thrived on the strategy involved in competition. He often wrote down the way that opposing pitchers pitched and other nuances of the game in a little black notebook. He could later consult his notes in order to improve his team's chances of winning the next time they faced that team. He took an intelligent approach to these otherwise raucous and loosely organized sports. Later in his storied career, Rickey's little black notebook would become famous to friends and opponents alike.

In 1902, Branch Rickey focused all of his athletic efforts on baseball. He rose through the semi-professional ranks as a catcher on several minor league teams. In 1903, he was promoted to the Cincinnati Reds, the team he loved most as a youth. But Branch Rickey's stay with the Reds was short, playing only one game on a Saturday afternoon. After the game, the manager told Rickey to report to the field the next day. (Sunday was the most profitable day of the week for baseball teams.) Rickey explained that he could not come to the field because of his religious convictions and the promise he had made to his mother. The coach immediately dismissed Rickey from the team in a humiliating fashion.

From 1904 to 1907, Rickey earned two bachelor degrees from Ohio Wesleyan and held down jobs as a coach and athletic director, first at

Allegheny College in Pennsylvania and later at his alma mater. He married his childhood sweetheart, Jane Moulton, during this time, and he also continued to play professional baseball for the St. Louis Browns. In 1907, he was traded to the New York Highlanders, the predecessor of the Yankees. However, he had burned the candle at both ends for several years, which showed in his slumping baseball statistics. His batting average was below .200, and he was unable to throw out runners as they attempted to steal bases. He once allowed a record-setting thirteen bases stolen in one nine-inning game. Rickey left professional baseball late in 1907, and once again he took a job in Ohio teaching Latin and coaching football and baseball at Ohio Wesleyan.

Once in this familiar university setting, the brilliant twenty-six-year-old Rickey contemplated his career path. He had become an accomplished orator as a schoolteacher and a strong proponent of the Prohibitionist movement, which sought to outlaw the making, selling and buying of alcoholic beverages. At the urging of friends, he seriously considered entering politics. But his passion for sports was stronger than his desire for public office. Then, in 1909, Rickey's health suddenly failed. He was diagnosed with tuberculosis. After six months' rest, he returned to work coaching football and baseball and studying law, this time at the University of Michigan. In just two years he earned his law degree.

But these were pivotal years in Branch Rickey's development for another reason. At the time, college athletic teams were integrated, and the University of Michigan's baseball team had a black player named Charley Thomas. In 1910, when the team traveled to Indiana for a game, the hotel manager registered all but Thomas. Rickey threatened to take the whole team elsewhere, but then the manager offered a compromise: Thomas could room with Rickey. Rickey gave the young black ballplayer his room key and went to get the rest of the team settled in. When he returned to his room, he had a life-changing experience. Rickey told the story decades later to sportscaster Red Barber:

When I opened the door I saw Charley. He was sitting on the edge of a chair. He was crying. He was pulling at his hands as though he would tear the very skin off.

"It's my skin, Mr. Rickey... it's my skin! If I could just pull it off I'd be like everybody else... It's my skin, Mr. Rickey."

That was forty-one years ago. And for these forty-one years I have heard that fine young man crying, "It's my skin, Mr. Rickey... If I could just pull it off... It's my skin."

Now I'm going to do something about it.

This experience shocked Rickey and ignited within him a passion to fight racism in the game of baseball that would take four decades to complete.

It was no surprise to those who knew Branch Rickey when, after a brief stint practicing law, he headed straight back into baseball. Bob Hedges, who had been Rickey's boss when he was with the St. Louis Browns, hired him as a coach and part-time scout. Hedges was impressed with the detailed scouting reports, his keen knowledge of the game, and his uncanny ability to analyze baseball prospects. With the Browns stuck in the American League cellar, Hedges was thoroughly disgusted with two previous managers that season. He put Rickey in charge for the last eleven games of 1914. Rickey lifted the Browns out of the cellar and brought them to a fifth-place finish.

After the Browns were sold in 1916, Rickey was forced out of the dugout and into the front office. It was a blessing in disguise. His approach to the game of baseball always had been cerebral. He often lectured his players on baseball theory and strategy. Once away from the dugout, Rickey focused on rebuilding the team by acquiring more talented players. His first strategy was to create what would later become the "farm system," arguably baseball's greatest innovation. This system placed surplus players on friendly minor league ballclubs where they could get further training. Likewise, the best of the players on these farm teams could be purchased by major league teams for bargain prices. It took several years, but this system proved extremely fruitful, and Rickey's skills as a master strategist were becoming known to a larger audience of baseball executives.

Branch Rickey also was becoming more widely known for his high standards and principles. While he was managing, he had it written into his contract that he would not manage Sunday games. He never used profane language, and he abstained from alcohol. He was known as a straight arrow and players and executives routinely ridiculed him for his moral convictions. One sportswriter dubbed Rickey "The Mahatma," a reference to Mahatma Gandhi, the Indian peace activist and leader. Because he was so found of pontificating on baseball and life, his office was known by reporters as the "cave of winds." "He was a man of many faucets, all turned on," another quipped.

After the 1916 season, Rickey moved from the American League Browns to the National League St. Louis Cardinals to become the team's president. Rickey now was firmly entrenched in the business of baseball. As president of the Cardinals, he produced a third-place team in 1917, anchored by a young star named Rogers Hornsby. After a couple of disappointing seasons, he concluded that the farm system would have to pay bigger dividends with the Cardinals. He started by buying part ownership in many minor league teams. When competition for good players increased, he began buying them outright. The Cardinals' sole ownership of these farm teams gave them a lock on the talent pool. Legendary baseball commissioner Judge Kenesaw Mountain Landis, however, decided in 1922 to prohibit baseball organizations from owning more than one team in any given minor league. By this time, though, "Farmer Rickey's produce" was already ripe. In 1926, the Cardinals set the league on fire. Hornsby, a .400 hitter, played and managed, and the Cardinals won their first pennant. They went on to beat the powerhouse New

York Yankees (who fielded Babe Ruth and Lou Gehrig, among other stars) in a seven-game World Series.

Becoming world champions propelled the Cardinals and Branch Rickey into the limelight. Rickey had a well-deserved reputation for making astute trades and for controlling team finances very tightly. The frugality of his youth had not left him, and he attempted to pass its lessons on to his team. He used salary negotiations as an opportunity to teach his players important moral lessons about temperance and restraint, earning him the nickname "the Deacon."

Rickey's motto was, "Education never stops," and he did his best to instill this principle throughout the Cardinals organization. His paternalistic style produced winners. In twenty-one seasons as general manager of the Cardinals, Rickey's ballclubs won nine pennants and six world championships. In 1942, Rickey's last year with the Cardinals, the team won a club-record 106 games and a World Championship. Also that year, Rickey, true to his vow in 1910, tried valiantly to integrate the stands at the Cardinals' Sportsman's Park. His efforts failed because owner Sam Braedon and manager Hornsby vehemently opposed the idea. They said it was bad for business.

Rickey's contract expired at the end of the 1942 season and Braedon did not renew it. The two men differed in opinion on many occasions, and although the strain in their relationship did not show on the ball field, it broiled behind the scenes. Even though he was already sixty-one, Rickey never considered retirement. He looked for a new ballclub, and the offers were plentiful. He chose the Brooklyn Dodgers who offered him a free hand in running the team and a $50,000 annual contract. Of Rickey's move east, a St. Louis sports editor noted that Rickey would not have the advantage in Brooklyn of a great farm system, but "those who know believe he'll find a way [to succeed], and baseball will experience another revolutionary innovation of some kind."

With America's entry into World War II late in 1941, Rickey's zeal for baseball combined with his patriotism. Though some Americans called for the major leagues to cancel all play, President Franklin D. Roosevelt thought it was in the best interest of the nation for baseball to go on. Rickey, in full support of Roosevelt, stated that Americans need to "hold on to such diversions as tend to relieve us from the ever-increasing sorrows of war." This speech became Brooklyn's battle cry. The strong emotion for Brooklyn and all of baseball to succeed in its new mission encouraged Rickey to approach the Brooklyn owners in 1943 about recruiting black players. Rickey contended that "a Negro player or two will not only help the Brooklyn organization, but putting colored players in the major leagues will also accomplish something that is long overdue. It is something I have thought about and believed in for a long time." World War II had struck the conscience of many other Americans who believed that if blacks were good enough to fight and die for their country, they were good enough to play in the major leagues. It became a popular cause, especially in New York City, during the later stages of the war.

The Dodgers' owners agreed, but they knew this innovation would be fraught with controversy from other teams, players and fans. In 1943, Rickey persuaded Dodger owners that this "experiment" could work if the right player or players were selected to integrate baseball. It would take a monumental scouting effort, one that would be international in scope and last for two years. No one suspected that Branch Rickey had already formulated a detailed plan to ensure that the integration of baseball would become a reality.

In 1919, while Branch Rickey's professional baseball career was in full swing, one of the best baseball players in history was born. Jackie Robinson was born in Cairo, Georgia, the last of five children. When Jackie was six months old, his sharecropping father abandoned the family, leaving Jackie's mother, Mallie, to raise the children alone. Without adequate means of providing for her young family, Mallie packed their belongings and moved all six Robinsons to southern California in 1920. There they lived with aunts, uncles and cousins, totaling thirteen in one small apartment. Shortages of food and other necessities were the norm. Mallie Robinson worked hard doing domestic work and eventually earned enough money to afford a small but comfortable house. The home was in an all-white neighborhood in Pasadena. The white neighbors attempted to force the Robinsons out, but Mallie did not budge—her determination to stay was unwavering. Her youngest son would later display the same kind of determination in life and baseball.

The Robinsons lived just minutes from the site of the Rose Bowl, where young Jackie loved to chase rabbits. His fascination with athletics began in the schoolyard, and he was the best at most of the games played. His quickness, strength, and ability to concentrate showed early in his life, but so did his propensity for mischief. As a youth, he was a member of the Pepper Street Gang, a collection of black, Mexican and Japanese kids. This group of energetic kids threw dirt clods at cars, committed petty theft, and generally created a nuisance. Robinson later credited a young minister named Karl Downs for keeping him out of trouble. Reverend Downs was a remarkable communicator and made church attendance for young people, including Jackie Robinson, a pleasure rather than a duty. Mallie's prayers for her youngest son's well-being were answered through Karl Downs's lasting friendship.

From the time Jackie Robinson was in junior high school, he excelled at four sports: football, basketball, baseball and track. His family, especially his brothers Frank and Mack, always encouraged him. Despite a heart condition, Mack Robinson was a superb track star. He finished second to Jesse Owens in the 200 meters at the Berlin Olympics in 1936. In high school, Jackie helped Muir Tech win many championships, sometimes almost single-handedly. He took his talents first to Pasadena Junior College, where in one day he set a new running broad jump record of 25 feet 6-1/2 inches, and led his baseball team to the championship. At UCLA, Robinson became the school's first four-sport letterman. Sportswriters began calling him "the Jim Thorpe of his race," a reference to the Native American athlete who became the 1912 Olympic decathlon gold medalist, as well as a star professional football and baseball player. But Robinson left UCLA after two years. He needed to help his mother financially and felt "no amount of education would help a black man get a job. I felt I was living in an academic and athletic dream world."

In the late 1930s, while sports occupied Jackie Robinson's life, a friendship with a female student, Rachael Isum, took control of his heart. When Robinson left UCLA in 1940 prior to completing his degree, he continued to court Rachel while he looked for a job in his chosen field of athletics. He became an assistant athletic director for the New Deal's National Youth Administration, working with kids from poor or broken homes. He found the work extremely rewarding, but the NYA shut down when war broke out in Europe.

Robinson gave professional football a try. Football was his best sport, but the only league that allowed black players was in Hawaii. Never one to let a minor inconvenience keep him from competing, he crossed the Pacific Ocean and played professionally for the Honolulu Bears in the fall of 1941. He also worked for a construction company during the week. The 1941 football season ended in November, and Robinson boarded an ocean liner bound for southern California on December 5, 1941. Two days later, the U.S. naval base Pearl Harbor was bombed by the Japanese, and the United States was thrust into World War II. The twenty-two-year-old Robinson enlisted in the Army, where he attained the rank of second lieutenant.

Two years of military service helped prepare Robinson for the skirmishes he would face on his own battlefield in sports. He had a fighting spirit attached to his righteous anger. He once telephoned a superior officer in order to acquire more seats in the base exchange for black soldiers. The officer responded by asking if Robinson would want his wife "sitting next to a nigger." Robinson reported that his rage took over, and he lit into the man over the phone at the top of his voice. In future dealings, that officer treated Robinson with respect.

On another occasion, Robinson sat near the front of an Army bus next to the wife of a fellow officer. They were friends. The bus driver, no doubt angered by the sight of a black man talking to a white woman, stopped the bus and ordered Robinson to go to the back of the bus. Encouraged by the example of Joe Louis, America's black boxing hero who underwent a similar experience in the Army, and by the Army's own liberal bus policy because of it, Robinson refused. The driver called the military police, and Robinson found himself that evening being interrogated by a racist officer and his female companion. As Robinson defended himself and pinpointed his interrogator's prejudice, he was accused of drunkenness and attempting to start a riot. Robinson admitted that he was naive as to how far some members of the Army would go to "put a vocal black man in his place. Everything would have been allright if I had been a 'yassuh boss' type." He was faced with court-martial proceedings but was exonerated. In November 1944, after more than two years of dedicated service, Robinson was honorably discharged from the Army. He was free to pursue an athletic career. He also would have more time to spend with Rachel, now his fiancée.

After the war, Jackie Robinson needed steady employment to provide for himself and his mother, and to save for his future with Rachel. He investigated professional baseball and took a job in the only league that was available to black players, the Negro League. His team, the Kansas City Monarchs, gave him a contract paying $400 a month, a bonanza for Robinson. He was elated even though a white player of Robinson's caliber would have made much more in the major leagues.

Robinson began spring training in 1945 with the Monarchs. The realities of the road trips, the grueling schedule, and lack of adequate food and accommodations made him wonder about his athletic future. The reality of America in the 1940s did not include an opportunity for blacks to play in the major leagues with the best white players. As a competitor, Robinson could not experience what his brother Mack had in the 1936 Olympics when he represented America against the best runners in the world, regardless of race. Reflecting on this harsh reality in his autobiography, *I Never Had It Made*, Robinson states:

> *In those days a white ballplayer could look forward to some streak of luck or some reward for hard work to carry him into prominence or even stardom. What had the black player to hope for?... I felt unhappy and trapped. If I left [Jim Crow] baseball, where could I go, what could I do to earn enough money to help my mother and to marry Rachel?... The solution to my problem was only days away in the hands of a tough, shrewd, courageous man called Branch Rickey.*

And concerning Branch Rickey, Robinson continued:

> *I had read about him.... If I ever thought about him, even vague-*

ly, I probably would have assessed him as one of the powerful clique which was keeping baseball lily-white. If any one had told me that there was a ghost of a memory in this man's life which had haunted him for years and would be a prime cause in Mr. Rickey's deciding to challenge Jim Crow baseball, I would have thought it all a fantasy. Further, if someone had predicted that Mr. Rickey's momentous decision would involve me and change the whole course of my life and the course of sports in America, I would have called the predictor insane.

Jackie Robinson was unaware of the chain of events that began in 1943, quietly and behind the scenes in meetings between baseball owners and executives, which would change professional baseball forever. He also had no clue that he would be the instrument of such a sports drama, a drama that would become known as "The Noble Experiment."

The owners' decision to drop the color bar in baseball began ostensibly in 1943, but its first test failed in Philadelphia at the hands of baseball Commissioner Landis. Landis had stated that, "Each club is entirely free to employ Negro players to any and all extents it desires. The matter is solely for each club's decision, without restriction whatsoever," but this was merely a public-relations stunt. This became clear in 1943 when Bill Veeck Jr., the brazen son of the president of the Chicago Cubs, attempted to buy the Philadelphia Phillies and stock it with black players. Landis used all of his vast powers to arrange for someone else to buy the club before Veeck could do so.

By 1945 the change to the whites-only policy had yet to be tested. Judge Landis died and a new commissioner was elected. Albert "Happy" Chandler had a much more liberal view toward blacks in the major leagues, particularly in light of the war effort. Still, various black stars occasionally tried out for Major League clubs but were never offered contracts. Branch Rickey was determined that his Dodgers would be the first to put a black man on a major league roster.

True to his deliberate and intelligent nature, Rickey formulated a six-step plan for implementing integration in the major leagues. First, he would gain the approval of the Brooklyn Dodgers' three owners; this was accomplished in 1943. Second, he needed to find just the right player. Third, the choice would need to have an extremely strong character to withstand the opposition he would encounter. Step four was to make news reporters aware of the decision. He held a private meeting with Red Barber, a southerner who was the radio voice of the Dodgers. Fifth, he included and solicited the help of black community leaders. And finally, Branch Rickey prepared the Brooklyn players for the new man by stating that if anyone had a problem with it he could find employment elsewhere.

In addition to the six-step plan, Rickey also thought to devise a smokescreen so that his scouts could visit black teams and not be questioned. He announced the formation of the Brooklyn Brown Dodgers team in an all-new Negro league. This incited the black press particularly, as it seemed that yet again a white man was going to exploit black athletes. They did not suspect that it was a ploy.

Rickey also enlisted the help of Dr. Dan Dodson, a sociologist associated with the mayor's office, to organize a committee to look into baseball integration. Because of World War II's demands on blacks, race riots in Harlem in 1943, and an anti-discrimination law, New York's mayor, Fiorello La Guardia, was eager to have baseball drop the color line in order to ease mounting racial tension. "Organizing a committee" typically slows down a process, and this was Rickey's goal: the committee would stall the impatient city officials so that Rickey could carry out the six steps to integration in the way he had been planning for years.

Between 1943 and 1945, Branch Rickey searched and scouted diligently for just the right player. He spent $25,000 to find the best black man to lead off. He decided on the extremely talented and unsuspecting Robinson and was ready to offer him this pivotal position. It was Robinson's stellar play, his intelligence, service in the military, and strong moral character that made him the choice.

Dodger scout Clyde Sukeforth approached Jackie Robinson at Comiskey Park in Chicago before a Kansas City Monarchs game. (Black teams often rented Major League parks, which gave team owners a financial incentive to resist integration and maintain separate leagues.) They traveled together to Brooklyn, and Sukeforth introduced Robinson to Rickey. He described the feeling in the room as electric.

Jackie Robinson was not prepared for the startling opportunity Rickey presented him. Rickey told Robinson that he had been selected, after an exhaustive search, to be the first black in the major leagues. Although he was taken completely off guard, Robinson's life had in many ways prepared him for this challenge. Branch Rickey proved his sincerity to Robinson by offering him a salary of $5,000 and a $3,500 signing bonus.

As Rickey spoke to Robinson that August day in 1945, he readied him for the insults, indignation, hatred, and even death threats that were sure to confront him in Major League Baseball. He role-played with Robinson, acting as the angry and bitter white fan or player who might carry out these behaviors. "How do you like that, nigger boy," he taunted Robinson, pretending to be an opposing player who just had spiked him. Rickey's extensive scouting report on Robinson showed he had the guts to stand up for himself, but Rickey wanted him to have "the guts not to fight back." He explained that many people were looking for an excuse to prevent the success of the experiment. After all the role-playing and admonitions, Robinson wondered if he really could "turn the other cheek.... I did not know how I would do it. Yet I knew that I must. I had to do it for so many reasons. For black youth, for my mother, for myself. I had already begun to feel I had to do it for Branch Rickey." The noble and self-sacrificing spirit had gripped both men.

Two months later, on October 23, 1945, the handsome star athlete officially signed with the Dodgers' top farm club, the International League Montreal Royals. The eyes of the world would be on Robinson, waiting for him to make the smallest mistake. Robinson's every action would dictate how the nation felt about blacks mixing with whites in the sporting arena and in general. After completing more training with Mr. Rickey, Robinson headed for the Dodgers' farm club in Montreal to gain invaluable experience on the field.

Ample evidence proves that both participants in this Noble Experiment had much to lose and placed their personal reputations on the line. Rickey's family feared for the sixty-four year old's health and the way he would be maligned further in the press. Rickey's son, nicknamed Twig, thought southern prospects would shun Brooklyn. But the main assault came in the questioning of Rickey's financial motives. Many thought the Brooklyn general manager was merely looking to line his pockets with increased black attendance and cared nothing about the injustices. There was as much evidence that he actually could have been destroyed financially, since white fans might have stopped attending out of protest. Minor league baseball commissioner William Bramham sarcastically remarked that "we can expect a Rickey Temple to be in the course of construction in Harlem soon.... It is those of the carpetbagger stripe of the white race, under the guise of helping but in truth using the Negro for their own selfish interests, who retard the race."

Rickey's announcement caught other baseball officials and owners off guard. Some minor league presidents begged Rickey not to have Robinson play on their home fields for fear of negative press and unrest, and they even predicted bloodshed. Rogers Hornsby, Rickey's longtime associate in St. Louis and a staunch opponent to integration, doubted if ballplayers of both races could live together on the road—a criticism quickly dismissed by most since it had occurred regularly on college teams. (St. Louis was the last ballclub to integrate its stands.) Although Rickey stated he just wanted to win ballgames with the best players, he later revealed, "I couldn't face my God much longer knowing that His black creatures are held separate from His white creatures in the game that has given me all I own."

When Robinson signed, he was quoted in the *Montreal Herald* as saying, "Guess I'm just a guinea pig in this noble experiment." He expressed hope that he could use this athletic opportunity to do something for his entire race. In the black press, there was jubilation and much congratulation for Branch Rickey and Jackie Robinson. But Ludlow Werner, editor of the *New York Age*, summed up the weight that the twenty-six-year-old star would bear:

> *I'm happy over the event, but I'm sorry for Jackie. He will be haunted by the expectations of his race. To 15,000,000 Negroes he will symbolize not only their prowess in baseball, but their ability to rise to an opportunity. Unlike white players, he can never afford an off day or an off night. His private life will be watched too, because white America will judge the Negro race by everything he does. And Lord help him with his fellow Negroes if he should fail them.*

Jackie Robinson put his dignity on the line and had everything to lose. Beginning with his first spring training in Florida in 1946, he encountered all the usual Jim Crow humiliations. There had been twenty-six lynching attempts against blacks that year in Florida. Officials there refused to allow Robinson to play in exhibition games and even padlocked the parks. Other games were cancelled in the south for fear of crowd reactions. It was an eye-opening experience for Robinson and for Rachel, who was now his wife. Robinson heeded Rickey's advice about keeping quiet in this, the first and harshest test of his organized baseball career. Rachel Robinson remembers that it was "particularly painful for Jackie, because he was such an assertive person and was very sure of his manhood.... To have to see him kowtow and submit to these indignities was abominable." Once Branch Rickey signed Robinson, he too fought battles behind the scenes with owners and managers, but he never stepped into the skirmishes that Robinson had to face with his entrance into organized ball.

Although the Robinsons were very welcome in their new city of Montreal, the team still encountered opposition in other cities in the league. Rickey purposely placed Robinson in Montreal, knowing that the southernmost city they played would be Baltimore. It was there that boos, death threats, and fan violence threatened to erode the experiment. After one game there, a fight broke out at home plate. Fans poured out of the stands and it took several units of police to clear the field. Fortunately, Robinson had already reached the locker room, but an angry crowd followed him and surrounded the doors until about one o'clock in the morning. Ironically, two southern teammates stayed with Robinson until the crowd finally dispersed and then they escorted him back to his hotel on a city bus.

According to his agreement with Rickey, Robinson had to ignore the constant jeers, profanity and insults from opposing benches and managers. Robinson was brushed back and hit with many pitches. Certain managers reportedly ordered their pitchers to hit Robinson, and one even offered to buy a new suit for anyone who could knock him down. He played second base, where many base runners ran at him aggressively in an attempt to knock him down and otherwise impair his play. He took spikes in his legs. Under normal circumstances, a white player would have been justified either to fight back or at least unleash anger on the opponent. But Jackie Robinson, always composed, knew that much more was at stake than his personal pride and graciously explained the assaults as just part of the game.

Montreal finished the 1946 season in the Little World Series against the Louisville Colonels. Robinson again was treated harshly by the road crowds. The Colonels jumped out to a series lead of two games to none. But the noble play of Robinson, whose hitting and fielding brought his team back to win the next four games, led them to the championship. The Montreal fans chased him, hugged and kissed him out of pure love, and lifted their hero onto their shoulders.

After winning over the city of Montreal with his tremendous ability and winning personality in 1946, Robinson was elevated to the "bigs" in Brooklyn for the 1947 season. Although he had not only survived but triumphed in the minors, acceptance in the major leagues would have to be earned separately. Notified only one week prior to the season opener, Robinson assumed his new position at first base in order not to upset the talented Dodger lineup. He learned later that some of the players on the Dodgers had circulated a petition against Robinson's promotion. It was discovered by Rickey, who immediately called a meeting and threatened the plotters with termination. The movement was aborted quickly.

It was not until the Dodgers played a home game against the Philadelphia Phillies that their true loyalty to the new first baseman would be tested. The opposing dugout went way beyond even baseball's standard for verbal assaults and baiting. The manager of the club, Ben Chapman, was most at fault. Fans sitting nearby wrote letters of complaint and called for punishment. Chapman was known for his racial insults to Jews and Polish players in the past, but he surpassed himself at this game. Jackie Robinson relayed how this was almost his breaking point in self-restraint.

> *I have to admit that this day...brought me nearer to cracking up than I ever had been. I felt tortured and I tried just to play ball and ignore the insults.... What did Mr. Rickey expect of me? I was, after all, a human being. What was I doing here turning the other cheek as though I weren't a man? I thought what a glorious, cleansing thing it would be to let go. Then, I thought of Mr. Rickey—how his family and friends had begged him not to fight for me and my people. I thought of all his predictions, which had come true. Mr. Rickey had come to a crossroads and made a lonely decision. I was at a crossroads. I would make mine. I would stay.*

Eddie Stanky, a Dodger teammate who originally was cool to Robinson, publicly defended Robinson against the Phillies dugout. Though it did not stop the assaults, it was pivotal in making Robinson a true member of the Dodgers. That led to increased press coverage that lauded Robinson's manhood and composure.

Early in the 1947 season, when the St. Louis Cardinals came to Brooklyn, it was rumored that Branch Rickey's former team and biggest rival would go on strike rather than take the field with a black man. The other major league teams could easily have jumped on the bandwagon. Whether or not a strike conspiracy existed, it forced baseball executives to take a stand once and for all on the issue. Commissioner Happy Chandler and Ford Frick, the National League president, stood firmly behind Rickey and Robinson.

The ripple effect of Branch Rickey's Noble Experiment quickly reached the Dodger locker room. Six weeks into the season, the Brooklyn Dodgers had fully accepted their new black teammate. They ate together, talked, and played cards. Pee Wee Reese, a Kentucky-born shortstop, developed the closest relationship with Robinson. At a Boston Braves game, Reese walked over to Robinson and placed his arm on his shoulder to discuss some strategy. This gesture silenced the Braves' bench, which had been tormenting Reese for playing beside a black man.

After a slow start that season, Jackie Robinson was voted Rookie of the Year and played with the confidence of a veteran in the field and at bat. He led the league in stolen bases and played in more games than any other Dodger. He was hit with a pitched ball more than any other player in 1947. He led his team to the National League pennant and became the first black player to appear in a World Series. Though the Dodgers lost to the powerhouse Yankees, their crosstown rivals, Robinson played spectacularly. Most importantly, he handled himself with dignity despite the horrendous insults, the hate mail, the physical abuse, and the loneliness he endured.

Robinson's best year in baseball was probably 1949. He was voted the National League's Most Valuable Player, and he led the Dodgers to another pennant. It also was the year that Branch Rickey told Robinson that he was on his own to react freely on the field as he, Robinson, saw fit. He had proven himself to a national audience as having self-control, pride and class. Most other teams had contracted black players and the Dodgers had added others, including star catcher Roy Campenella and pitching ace Don Newcombe. Although Rickey signed the first five black players, he purposely left many players in the talent pool. Other teams followed Brooklyn's lead.

Jackie Robinson went on to have a great career. He was elected to the Hall of Fame in Cooperstown, New York, in 1962, his first year of eligibility. His Hall of Fame plaque reads:

Jack Roosevelt Robinson
Brooklyn N.L. 1947–1956

Leading N.L. batter in 1949. Holds fielding mark for second base-
man playing 150 or more games with .992. Led N.L. in stolen
bases in 1947 and 1949. Most Valuable Player in 1949. Lifetime
batting average .311. Joint record holder for most double plays
by second baseman, 137 in 1951. Led second basemen in double
plays 1949-50-51-52.

Branch Rickey was also inducted into the Hall of Fame, and his
plaque reads:

Wesley Branch Rickey
St. Louis A.L. 1905-1906-1914
New York A.L. 1907

Founder of farm system which he developed for St. Louis Car-
dinals and Brooklyn Dodgers. Copied by all other major league
teams. Served as executive for Browns, Cardinals, Dodgers and
Pirates. Brought Jackie Robinson to Brooklyn in 1947.

That last phrase reveals volumes about the life and character of
Branch Rickey. He and Jackie Robinson remained close long after their
baseball days were over. Jackie Robinson called Rickey "the father he
never had." Rickey dignified Robinson by never accepting any honors or
awards for signing Robinson and insisting that The Noble Experiment
was not to be commercialized, politicized, or over-dramatized.

In Cooperstown, Robinson and Rickey are recognized for their contributions to baseball, but they will be remembered for their combined
ability to alter the moral fabric of America. From very different backgrounds, but sharing the same noble spirit, these heroes resolutely took
the nation into uncharted territory. The integrated ballfield allowed
men to be judged on how honorably they played the game, and it forced
a nation to begin to admit its hypocrisy. In the face of entrenched op-

position, Branch Rickey and Jackie Robinson, through the national pastime, led America into the future.

The day after Rickey died, an editor at the *New York Times* wrote that among Branch Rickey's many exceptional qualities the most important was vision. "He had the ability, rare in any field and all but nonexistent in baseball, of seeing clearly the shape of the future.... This major step toward desegregation in an intensively publicized sector of our society... preceded comparable advances in most other areas of national life.... His genius and courage lay in recognizing the right time to proceed.... He was a baseball man through and through, but he exerted an influence far beyond that sport. He left his stamp on the minds of hundreds of the men who continue to work in baseball and, through them, his stamp on American culture."

True Nobility
True nobility is exempt from fear.
—William Shakespeare, Henry VI

Facts of the Matter
A Legacy of Scholarship and Leadership

In 1973, to honor her husband's memory, Rachel Robinson established the Jackie Robinson Foundation (JRF). The Foundation's mission statement makes its main goal clear: "Serving as an advocate for young people with the greatest need, the Foundation assists increasing numbers of minority youths through the granting of four-year scholarships for higher education." In the 2006-2007 school year the JRF supported 266 scholars. Applicants are selected on the basis of academic ability, financial need, and leadership potential.

At the heart of the JRF is the recognition that it takes more than money for a student to reach his or her full potential. It also takes mentoring and the maintenance of ongoing support relationships with the scholarship recipients. Each recipient participates in the JRF's Education and Leadership Development Program to build these relationships and to create networks of opportunity.

The JRF has also created a program called Extra Innings to further help scholarship recipients in overcoming obstacles to achieving graduate education and other advanced training.

To learn more about the Jackie Robinson Foundation, visit its website at www.jackierobinson.org.

PERSISTENCE

Althea Gibson

Althea Gibson grew up a tomboy in New York City in the 1930s. She survived her poor Harlem upbringing by playing sports of all types: basketball, football, baseball, and eventually paddle tennis and racquet tennis. She played as well as or better than most boys her age. When times were roughest for her at home, playing sports became her refuge. She began to play tennis with a passion and developed an inner drive "to be somebody." A lengthy period of failures nearly caused Gibson to quit tennis the year before her greatest international victory brought her worldwide fame. Her dream came true, though, because of the persistent effort and belief that she could achieve excellence.

❧·❧

Althea Gibson was born August 25, 1927, in Silver, South Carolina. She was the first of five children born to Daniel and Annie Gibson, who scratched out a living by sharecropping cotton. After ruinous weather destroyed most of one year's harvest, Daniel Gibson moved his family to Harlem in New York City. There, living with his Aunt Sally, he started a new life. He immediately got a job as a handyman in a mechanic's garage making ten dollars a week, a sum that made him feel rich compared to the seventy-five dollars he had made for a whole year sharecropping. The Gibson family moved into their own apartment several years later, not far from Aunt Sally.

The hustle and bustle of Harlem made Althea restless. She enjoyed being outdoors and especially liked competition. She sought an outlet in a multitude of games. Any game that the neighborhood boys played, she made sure to play—and she proved herself a worthy opponent in all of them. Early on, she showed great hand-eye coordination, especially evident on the baseball diamond. Gibson also had grit and strength, most noticeable in football games. Her father, though he was a newcomer to New York, wasn't naive about the battles his children might have to fight to survive in an urban environment. An avid sportsman himself, he taught Althea how to box. He taught her to "always get in the first punch."

Toughness was something Daniel Gibson demanded of his children, and he was strict with them. While Althea used what she learned from her father to survive and even thrive on the street, she became, as she called herself in her autobiography, "a wild, arrogant girl" in her teens. Her father's brand of corporal discipline caused her to stay away from home as much as possible. She became independent as a teenager and often wound up spending more time at friends' houses than her own. The more time Althea spent "hanging out," the more mischief she got into, such as stealing food or candy. The more mischievous she became, the more her father punished her. It turned into a vicious cycle that she felt helpless to break. Instead, she ran.

After graduating from junior high school, Althea Gibson wandered from place to place and took on odd jobs to buy food. She avoided the pain of going home. In her most trying moments after junior high school, she deeply resented her father, but years later she said, "I deserved it [punishment]. I gave him a whole lot of trouble. I don't hate him for anything today. In fact, I love him. Somebody had to knock a little sense into me, and it wasn't easy." The New York Welfare Department provided young Althea with money and shelter, but when Althea did not meet their requirements, such as steady schooling and employment, they withdrew their support. At a grim do-or-die moment when her world seemed hopeless and without direction, Althea met Buddy Walker, who helped redirect her life. Walker worked for the parks department and had noticed Gibson's athletic talent playing paddle tennis. She showed enough promise that he gave her a pair of second hand regulation tennis racquets to see how she'd do in the more popular net sport. Walker's encouragement greatly boosted her confidence, which she then used to her advantage. Meeting a person she trusted outside her own family led Althea Gibson down a path toward success. Her will to succeed surfaced, and the fighter's spirit she showed in Harlem street contests now helped her win tennis matches.

At the age of fourteen, with strong supporters such as Walker and others, Gibson's world revolved around sport more than ever. In some of her earliest tennis matches at Harlem's all-black Cosmopolitan Club, Althea wanted to fight her opponent, with her fists if she were losing a match. But with patient coaching from Walker, her behavior improved. "I began to understand that you could walk out on the court like a lady, all dressed up in immaculate white, be polite to everybody, and still play like a tiger and beat the liver and lights out of the ball," Gibson recalled.

There soon were others involved in Althea Gibson's development as a tennis player and as a person. Fred Johnson, a well-regarded coach of other black athletes, assisted Gibson and helped mold her game. Off the court, a woman named Rhoda Smith befriended Gibson and gave her a place to live. Her own daughter had died, so she took Gibson under her wing, in a sense "adopting" her. Mrs. Smith observed Gibson's impetuous on-court behavior and commented, "Althea had played in the street all her life, and she just did not know any better." The nurturing home life Mrs. Smith provided Althea was reflected in her more positive and gracious demeanor on the tennis court.

Althea Gibson won the first tournament in which Fred Johnson entered her: the 1942 New York State Open Girl's Championship hosted by the Cosmopolitan Club. It was one of the few times she had the opportunity to play against a white girl, and they played for the championship. "I can't deny that [beating a white opponent] made the victory all the sweeter to me," she said. Tennis, like most sports at the time, was mostly segregated. Blacks were not allowed to play on all-white courts or in all-white clubs. Blacks had their own national tennis association, the American Tennis Association (ATA), to showcase the best black talent in the country. Althea Gibson lost in the girls' ATA finals in 1943, but won in 1944 and 1945. Her talent was unmistakable.

In 1945, the year Gibson turned eighteen, she formed a lasting friendship that would change her life. Through a girlfriend, Althea met the great boxer Sugar Ray Robinson and his wife, Edna Mae. They met in a bowling alley, and the brash Gibson's first words to the boxing champion were, "I can beat you bowling right now!" He liked her confidence, and the Robinson house soon became Gibson's home away from home. But she still wrestled with the question of what to do with her own life. After spending time with the Robinsons, though, she knew more than ever that she "wanted to be somebody."

Doors started to open in the tightly-knit black tennis community as Gibson's talent shone. Shortly after losing in the finals of her first ATA women's (over eighteen) championship, she received an invitation from two prominent black Southern doctors to train more intensively at their expense. She wisely accepted their offer and moved to Wilmington, North Carolina, to live with Dr. Hubert Eaton and his family. He owned the only court in Wilmington where blacks could play. Dr. Robert Johnson of Lynchburg, Virginia, the same coach who was so influential in Arthur Ashe's life, coached her and helped with her expenses. It was through the tutelage of Eaton and Johnson that Althea Gibson realized that not simply tennis, but also education would help her become somebody. Her tennis reflected their influence—she won the ATA women's championship in 1947 and for each of the following nine years. She showed their influence in academics as well, as she graduated tenth in her class from Wilmington Industrial High School in

1949. At graduation time, she responded excitedly about her academic accomplishment, but she was compelled to do more: "I was ready to break loose and have a little fun, but I was dead serious about making something out of my life."

Gibson received a scholarship to Florida A & M University, which allowed her dual avenues for success, but her tennis game paved the road to fame. Gibson's game, which utilized her size of almost six feet and her strength, quickness, and powerful serve, thrust her into the national limelight. Though she lost in the National Indoors Championship to a formidable opponent, Nancy Chaffee, in 1949 and 1950, she surprised many observers who doubted a black athlete could play at her level. About her budding tennis career and its role in elevating awareness of racial issues, Gibson said: "I have never regarded myself as a crusader. I try to do the best I can in every situation I find myself in, and naturally I'm always glad when something I do turns out to be helpful and important to all Negroes—or, for that matter, to all Americans, or maybe only to all tennis players."

The sport of tennis, and sports in general, had much to learn from Althea Gibson, but it took help from friends and admirers. She craved acceptance on her own merits, but this had been largely denied her at the highest level of national tennis. The United States Lawn Tennis Association (USLTA), the organization responsible for the nation's most prestigious event, the U.S. Nationals at Forest Hills, New York, paid little attention to Gibson's achievements, and threatened not to issue her the well-deserved invitation she needed to participate in the tournament. A former champion, Alice Marble, stood up for Althea Gibson to the white tennis establishment. Marble wrote a scathing editorial in the July 1950 issue of *American Lawn Tennis* magazine:

> *I think it's time we faced a few factors. If tennis is a game for ladies and gentlemen, it's also time we acted like gentlepeople and less like sanctimonious hypocrites. If there is anything left in the name of sportsmanship, it's more than time to display what it means to us. If Althea Gibson represents a challenge to the present crop of women players, it's only fair that they should meet the challenge on the courts, where tennis is played. I know those girls, and I can't think of one who would refuse to meet Miss Gibson in competition.... The entrance of Negroes into national tennis is as inevitable as it has proven in baseball, in football, or in boxing; there is no denying so much talent. The committee at Forest Hills has the power to stifle the efforts of one Althea Gibson, who may or may not be succeeded by others of her race who have equal or superior ability. They will knock at the door as she has done. Eventually the tennis world will rise up en masse to protest the injustices perpetrated by our policy-makers.*

Shortly after the editorial was published, Gibson later recalled, "the dam broke" and her career took off.

Just two weeks later, the Eastern Grass Court Championships, in South Orange, New Jersey, accepted Gibson's application to play in the event, which was second only to the Nationals in importance. Though she made it only to the second round (it was her first tournament on grass), the color bar in tennis had been broken. Then, in August 1950, she received word that she had been admitted to play in the U.S. Nationals "on her ability." A battle had been won in the courts of tennis power, but Althea Gibson's fight to prove that she was "somebody" was just beginning.

After an easy win in the first round at Forest Hills, Gibson faced Louise Brough, that year's Wimbledon champion, in the second round. With the match all even in sets, Gibson took the lead in the third and deciding set, 7-6. Then a huge thunderstorm postponed the completion of the match until the next day. The delay wore thin the already-frayed nerves of Althea Gibson. By the next morning, she "was a nervous wreck." It took Brough only ten minutes to dispose of her pressure-racked opponent. Gibson, though she was disappointed, took consolation in the fact that she more than held her ground against the world's best player. Sportswriter David Eisenberg commented, "I have sat in on many dramatic moments in sports, but few were more thrilling than Miss Gibson's performance against Miss Brough."

As stunning as Althea Gibson's rise to near the top of the world tennis rankings was, she had been languishing in her pursuit of true greatness for seven long years. Good things had happened in those years: graduation from Florida A & M; teaching physical education at Lincoln University in Jefferson City, Missouri; and continued coaching and support from key people (Sydney Llewellyn, her coach; and Joe Louis, the boxer, helped finance her). Regardless, Jet magazine labeled Gibson "the biggest disappointment in tennis" at one point during those years.

At several points in those troubled times, Gibson nearly put down her racquet for good, but she decided that tennis "still had a big hold on me." Ironically, a tour visiting and playing at Army bases in Southeast Asia in 1956 gave her the experience she needed to climb the final hurdle. After the tour, she entered eighteen tournaments around the world and won sixteen of them. She and others thought she was poised for the top. Again, nerves got the better of her at the 1956 Wimbledon championship. She lost in a grueling three-set match in the final to another American player, Shirley Fry, whom she had beaten earlier in a warm-up tournament. Gibson, who had begun to feel sorry for herself as well as for the friends, family, and supporters who stuck closely by her, realized she was trying too hard. "I wanted to win so badly, I pressed." Fry beat her again at Forest Hills that same year, 6-3, 6-4.

But all had not been lost in 1956, as Althea Gibson won the French Open, becoming the first black woman to win any of the four major tennis tournaments. She also won the Italian Open, this time defeating Fry 6-2, 6-4. But pressure mounted on Gibson to win the big ones that had eluded her for so long. Only a patient and persistent person such as Gibson could have pursued a dream to such lengths.

Althea Gibson, now an established veteran, went to Wimbledon in 1957. The tennis world finally recognized Gibson's talent. She anticipated a Wimbledon victory like a child anticipates Christmas. She knew inside it was hers to take, and she did so resoundingly, beating another American, Darlene Hard, in the finals. "At last! At last!" shouted Gibson as she ran to the net to shake hands with Hard. Telegrams of congratulations poured in from around the world, but especially from those who knew how much this victory meant for her and for them. At the Wimbledon Ball the evening after the championship, Gibson delivered a victory speech thanking all who had supported her over the years. She began: "In the words of your distinguished Mr. Churchill, 'This is my finest hour.' This is the hour I will remember always as the crowning conclusion to a long and wonderful journey." Near the end of her speech, she proclaimed:

> *And finally, this victory is a sincere thank-you to the many good people in England and around the world whose written and spo-*

ken expressions of encouragement, faith and hope I have tried to justify. No, my friends, this victory is a thing of no small matter. It is a total victory of many nations.

The exclamation point to her Wimbledon victory was a letter she received shortly after the tournament from President Dwight D. Eisenhower, which stated in part: "Many Americans, including myself, have watched with increasing admiration your sustained effort to win the heights in the tennis world.... Recognizing the odds you faced, we have applauded your courage, persistence and application.... You met the challenge superbly."

Althea Gibson had more fine hours in 1957 and beyond. She won the U.S. Nationals at Forest Hills that same year and repeated as champion in both events the following year. She climbed a rugged mountain on a path that led her to the top. She put everything she had into the sport she loved to play. Althea Gibson earned what she had wanted from a young age. She was somebody.

The Power of Persistence

Nothing in the world can take the place of persistence. Talent will not; nothing is more common than unsuccessful men with talent. Genius will not; unrewarded genius is almost a proverb. Education will not; the world is full of educated derelicts. Persistence and determination alone are omnipotent.

—President Calvin Coolidge

Facts of the Matter
Advancing Confidently in the Direction of Our Dreams

Henry David Thoreau (1817–1862) wrote in his classic book Walden, "If one advances confidently in the direction of his dreams, and endeavors to live the life which he has imagined, he will meet with a success unexpected in common hours." He was talking, of course, about persistence, and he, like Althea Gibson, knew well that it sometimes takes help from others to continue advancing confidently toward one's dreams.

The U.S. Athletic Trust was founded in the year 2000 to make it possible for potential Olympic athletes to continue working toward success. Recognizing that once such athletes leave college they are often without financial support for their continued training, the U.S. Athletic Trust, in the words of its mission statement, seeks to offer financing and mentoring, "thereby bringing to the top of their sport today's athletic achievers who will become society's leaders of tomorrow."

Since its founding, the U.S. Athletic Trust has helped many athletes—runners, discus-throwers, fencers, hockey players, and more—to persist in their following their dreams. Read more about it at www.usathletictrust.org.

DISCIPLINE

John Wooden

John Wooden played and coached basketball tenaciously. As a coach, he emphasized conditioning and teamwork. Fast-breaking offense designed to wear down the other team and tough defense keyed his teams' successes. The UCLA teams he coached won seven straight national championships from 1967 to 1973, and ten out of twelve from 1964 to 1975. Off the court, Wooden was a loyal husband and devoted father, and he lived by the highest moral standards in every area of his life.

⋙⋘

John Wooden was born October 14, 1910, in rural Hall, Indiana, the fourth and youngest of four boys born to Joshua and Roxie Wooden. The Wooden family farmed land Roxie had inherited from her parents. From a young age, John assisted his father, who worked at least twelve a day, six days a week, tending crops and livestock. Mr. Wooden taught his sons the importance of work and the role it played in keeping the farm productive. Sunday was always reserved as a day to rest and go to church. Mr. Wooden was a stern disciplinarian who corrected his son's misbehavior lovingly but firmly. John Wooden described his father as a man of "gentle strength" and "someone who would always be fair with me and had my best interests at heart." Roxie Wooden, according to John, "provided a role model for how to do my job regardless of the particular circumstances."

Sports were the best outlet for the Wooden boys. Their father also enjoyed sports, especially baseball, so he made sure he could participate in their fun. Because he and his son enjoyed baseball so much, Joshua Wooden cleared a section of farmland to make room for a baseball field.

He also built their first basketball goal out of a tomato basket. Mrs. Wooden produced the "ball" from discarded linens stuffed into old hosiery.

The Wooden household stressed education, too, and books were more prominent than sporting equipment. Mr. Wooden read and quoted books constantly. He passed on to his sons a love of literature and especially poetry. John Wooden would later say that his father "profoundly influenced me," especially in the area of learning. Joshua Wooden held his sons to a high standard, but he also provided them a living example. He did not ask of them more than he could model himself. He did not tolerate foolishness, wouldn't drink, smoke, use foul language, or speak harshly about another person. His steadfast rule was that if one couldn't say anything nice about a person, they shouldn't say anything at all.

John Wooden treasured his relationship with his father. For more than half a century he kept a little piece of paper in his wallet that his father had given him in grade school. It read:

1. *Be true to yourself.*
2. *Make each day your masterpiece.*
3. *Help others.*
4. *Drink deeply from good books, especially the Bible.*
5. *Make friendship a fine art.*
6. *Build a shelter against a rainy day.*
7. *Pray for guidance, count and give thanks for
   your blessings every day.*

John Wooden put his father's advice to good use. He studied hard and did well in school, played high school sports (football, basketball and baseball) with considerable success, and proved himself college material in an era when most high school graduates went to work rather than to college. He received a basketball scholarship offer to attend Purdue University in West Lafayette, Indiana, in 1928, but at that time there were no pure athletic scholarships. All scholarships and grants required working as well as playing a sport. Wooden worked a variety of jobs, including waiting tables and selling programs at football games, all four years to pay the tuition his parents couldn't afford.

On the court, Wooden excelled as a quick, playmaking guard. At 5 foot 10 inches in height and 180 pounds, he also scored his share of baskets, due in part to his tremendous leaping ability. Ward "Piggy" Lambert, Purdue's coach, relied heavily on Wooden's playmaking ability and "court sense." Purdue played a fast-breaking style, and Wooden's speed and finesse kept the offense running smoothly.

Coach Lambert and his star player had a special bond. Lambert saw in Wooden a unique individual, a true leader. Wooden admired Lambert for his coaching genius. During Wooden's sophomore year, Lambert offered him a total athletic scholarship (made available to Lambert by a West Lafayette doctor) that would allow him to study and play without having to work. For most of Purdue's athletes, that would have been a dream come true. Not for Wooden. He turned it down, knowing that without work he would feel as if he had not earned his education. Lambert respected Wooden's decision, and understood it had not even been a difficult one for him to make. Wooden was guided by the principle that he should earn his way and not settle for an easy or comfortable lifestyle handed to him on a silver platter. He hustled on and off the court to pay his way through college. He twice earned All-American honors in the process.

John Wooden was so good at basketball that kids throughout the state of Indiana, an emerging basketball hotbed, wanted to be like him. Said a former professional football player who had watched Wooden play at Purdue: "In my era, Wooden was to kids what Wilt Chamberlin or Kareem Abdul-Jabbar are today. He was a superstar, the idol of any kid who had a basketball. In Indiana, that was *every* kid." Despite his superstar status, John Wooden was intensely shy and quiet. Beneath that, however, there lurked a fierce competitor who hustled and scrapped all over the court, earning the nickname "The India Rubber Man." He would bounce, like a rubber ball, off other players and even walls in some of the smaller gyms, only to get right back into the action. His ability to bounce back proved helpful in another situation. He had dated Nellie Riley all through high school and college and planned to marry her after his graduation. But in the midst of the Great Depression in 1932, he lost all the money he had saved ($909.05) when his bank went out of business. He married Nell anyway, in 1932, penniless but very much in love.

Wooden's high school and college coaches had such a significant influence on him that he decided to coach after graduating from Purdue. Dayton High School in Dayton, Kentucky, gave him his start, inauspicious as it was. There he recorded his first and only losing season, but he forged a philosophy that served him well the rest of his lengthy career: "Get the players in the best of condition, and make them believe they are in better condition than our opponents so they won't fold in the second half. Teach them to execute the fundamentals quickly but without hurrying. Get them to play as a team, always thinking of passing the ball before shooting it."

A year after his Kentucky experience, he returned to his native state to coach South Bend Central High School, which soon became a basketball powerhouse. In eleven years at South Bend his record was 218 wins and 42 losses. He also extended his own playing career. He continued to play basketball, semi-professionally, for an Indianapolis-based team, and kept himself in peak physical condition.

John Wooden put his country ahead of his thriving career. When the United States entered World War II in 1941, Wooden, at the age of thirty-one, enlisted in the Navy. He spent three years as a physical education instructor for naval air troops and instilled in them the training and discipline they needed to win a contest far more important than a basketball game. When the war ended, Wooden returned to coaching at South Bend Central and then moved up a notch to the collegiate ranks two years later. Indiana State offered him a job when their coach, Wooden's own former high school coach, Glenn Curtis, resigned to take a job coaching professional basketball. It had been Curtis who mentored Wooden and taught him the mental toughness needed to win close ballgames. In Wooden's words, "He was one of the four most important men in my life."

Wooden's first Indiana State team went 18–7 and made the conference post-season tournament in Kansas City, Missouri. When the league refused to allow the lone black player on Indiana State's roster to play purely on the basis of his skin color, Wooden was outraged. He had witnessed Ku Klux Klan activity as a youth, and he was determined never to bow to racial hatred or discrimination. The player, Clarence Walker, was "not a great ballplayer," according to Wooden, and the team easily could have won without him. But Wooden's higher principles prevailed, and he removed his team from the tournament rather than compromise his belief in racial equality.

Wooden soon began to receive offers to coach "big time" college programs. His success became evident to a national audience of coaches and athletic administrators. In 1948, he was hired to head the program at UCLA in the powerful Pacific Coast Conference. UCLA had finished in last place the previous year, but Wooden was optimistic. He told an audience of boosters before his first season began, "We'll win fifty percent of our games by out-running the other team in the last five minutes." He exceeded his own wild prediction by winning twenty-two and losing only seven. He called that season "my most satisfying year of coaching" because he had taken a team with mediocre talent and made winners out of them. An observer called his team "uninhibited" and "blitzing." The very next year, their record of 24–7 was good enough to win the conference championship. Wooden's UCLA teams quickly made an impression on their opponents and gained national prestige.

Winning basketball games thrilled Wooden, his players, and UCLA fans everywhere. But Wooden's philosophy was not to win at any cost. Many times he was satisfied that "we've accomplished all we're capable of accomplishing, win or lose." His attitude was to dare his players to be great in basketball and life, and to put every ounce of strength into achieving their highest attainable goals. His focus was laser-like, but he never sacrificed his moral principles to gain success. He did not like recruiting players; he did not want to have undue influence on an important decision in any given player's life. In this aspect, Wooden admired Amos Alonzo Stagg, the college football coach who believed recruiting bred corruption. So he handed over most of UCLA's recruiting efforts to assistant coaches. While he toughened his players by working them hard in practice, he rarely punished his players in front of others. He said, "I try to work with players like doves. Some need to be held a little tighter.... Others don't need to be held as tightly.... Above all, a coach must be patient."

Referees and opposing players sometimes bore the brunt of Wooden's competitive character. He sometimes screamed at them from the bench, usually nothing more than a challenge to ensure fairness. His admonishments included absolutely nothing profane or indecent. His father had taught him better. "Yes. I yell at officials. I want my players to know I'm behind them." He, like his mentor, Glenn Curtis, became "a master psychologist," deriving the absolute best from his teams. His 1964 team proved that. His first national championship team, basketball's "Lilliputians" (no starter was taller than 6 foot 5 inches), won with "quickness and fanaticism"—the Wooden model.

Wooden's UCLA teams won better than eighty percent of their games during his twenty-eight years as coach. He became a legendary basketball teacher and strategist. He claimed he "was much more of a 'practice coach' than 'game coach,'" which meant that he drilled his teams in practice to handle instinctively the pressures of a game situation. They responded brilliantly, winning a total of 664 games while losing only 162.

Along the way, Wooden developed his "Pyramid for Success" as a teaching tool. In it, he defines success as "peace of mind which is a direct result of self-satisfaction in knowing you did your best to become the best that you are capable of becoming." Wooden's depth of understanding about the ingredients of success is evident on this very page. Wooden chose not to copyright his Pyramid for Success so that all coaches and teachers, athletes and spectators, could copy his work to gain inspiration.

Inspiration is what John Wooden gave to his players. His former superstar centers, Bill Walton and Kareem Abdul-Jabbar, attest to that. Said Walton: "Coach [Wooden] gained respect with a very simple method: by his personal example.... He never had to tell you that he was the one in charge or get up and give rah-rah speeches to get your attention. He led by being himself.... You saw how true he was to doing things right, by *thinking* right. Coach Wooden was more interested in the process than in the result." Abdul-Jabbar called Wooden a "fine man, a superb coach, and an honest and decent individual." Many other former players have achieved success in life because of the strong values and work ethic Wooden imparted to them. He once said "little things make big things happen," and his little deeds produced huge results.

Wooden's greatest asset was his inner strength. He wrote:

> *No coach should be trusted with the tremendous responsibility of handling young men under the great mental, emotional, and physical strain to which they are subjected unless he is spiritually strong. If he does possess this inner strength, it is only because he has faith and truly loves his fellow man.... Youngsters under his supervision will develop wholesome disciplines of body, mind, and spirit that will build character.*

When John's beloved wife, Nell, died in 1985, he fell into depression. His children, grandchildren, great-grandchildren, and friends rallied to his side. They helped revive his broken and grieving spirit. Over the course of several years, Wooden recovered, but he still visits his wife's grave almost every day. John Wooden made an indelible mark on athletics, creating a towering example for others to follow. His maxims about sports and life are etched in the minds of many athletes and coaches. Wooden continues to have an impact. Nearing the age of 100, he maintains a website, www.coachjohnwooden.com, from which he shares his philosophy and personal and professional histories.

John Wooden's many honors include being the first, and for more than twenty-five years the only, person elected to the Basketball Hall of Fame as both a player and coach. But his proudest achievements are his family and former players, not the accolades. "I'd like to be remembered as a good teacher and a good person, not as someone who won a lot of basketball championships," said Wooden. "I am just a common man who is true to his beliefs."

Our Greatest Wealth

But if one should guide his life by true principles, man's greatest wealth is to live on a little with contented mind; for a little is never lacking.

—Lucretius (99–55 BC)

Facts of the Matter
Athletes for a Better World

In 1998 a group of people dedicated to changing the culture of American athletics founded an organization called Athletes for a Better World (ABW). Led by Fred Northrup, ABW tries to bring out the positive values that lead to genuine sportsmanship and citizenship. ABW has developed a "Code for Living" that encourages athletes to:

- Work hard at their sport
- Demonstrate fair play
- Come together as one team
- Win or lose with grace and dignity
- Give something back to the community

It comes as no surprise that ABW chose to name it's annual award The Coach Wooden Citizenship Cup, given each year to a collegiate and a professional athlete "who have made the greatest difference in the lives of others." Past recipients include Peyton Manning and John Smoltz. The 2007 winners were John Lynch of the Denver Broncos and Anna Key, a goalkeeper for the University of California women's soccer team. More information about the ABW and the Coach Wooden Cup can be found online at www.abw.org.

TRIUMPH

Gertrude Ederle

Gertrude Ederle, an Olympic swimmer in the 1920s, had a remarkable athletic career. At one time, she held eighteen world records and in 1926 became the first woman ever to swim the English Channel. Health battles all but extinguished her storied career. But Ederle did not allow physical ailments to dampen her generous spirit. Her life after competitive sports proved that success can't be measured by the length or peak of one's sports career, but rather in how one triumphs over the obstacles put before them.

❦

Gertrude Ederle was born October 23, 1907 in New York City. She was the third of six children born to German immigrants Henry and Gertrude Ederle. "Trudy," as the younger Gertrude was called, grew up in a strict and disciplined home. She did many chores for her parents and worked in her father's butcher shop. The physical work gave Trudy a muscular physique.

From the age of nine, when her father first taught her how to swim, Trudy showed talent in the water. Her sister, Margaret, also a swimmer, encouraged her to swim competitively. The two joined a New York City swim club to race against other swimmers but also to get instruction on stroke techniques. There, Trudy learned the eight-beat crawl, a stroke that was created for speed and not style. At age thirteen, Trudy combined technique and natural strength to win a citywide junior event in the 100-yard freestyle. in 1922, she put her talent to an even greater test by entering her first long-distance race, the prestigious Joseph P. Day Cup, in the waters off Manhattan. There she demolished a field of fifty of the world's best swimmers and set a record for the three-and-a-half-

173

mile course. In her next event that same year, she shattered six world records in distances ranging from 150 yards to 500 meters. Despite her enormous early successes, she remained the shy, unassuming person that she had always been. Beneath the surface, however, lay a fierce competitor who readied herself for future challenges.

Leading up to the 1924 Olympics in Paris, Ederle won national championships at short distances (50 yards), long distances (one-half mile), and some in-between. She trained vigorously for the Summer Games, but fell short of expectations by winning only two bronze medals, in the 100- and 400-meter freestyles, and gold in the 400-meter freestyle relay. She made no excuses, though some observers thought her rigorous training actually might have hampered her performance.

True greatness lay beyond Paris for Trudy Ederle. After the Olympics, she began to concentrate on long-distance swimming. She set a record in a seventeen-mile swim from the Battery in lower Manhattan to Sandy Hook, New Jersey, completing the event in seven hours. Then Ederle set her sights on the most formidable of all distance swims—the English Channel. No woman had ever completed the twenty-one-mile endurance swim, though several had attempted it. Her first try, in August 1925, ended in failure after more than eight hours in the water. Unlike those who had preceded her in attempting the milestone swim, Ederle swam the entire distance doing the crawl stroke, a much more demanding technique (other Channel swimmers used the breast stroke). But she had not paced herself well enough to go the full distance. She attempted the Channel swim again the next summer. As she stood on the French shoreline near Calais, staring at the rough, cold seas she was about to enter, she calmly said, "Please God, help me."

For the next fourteen hours and thirty-one minutes, her body covered in several layers of the grease, lard, and petroleum jelly that endurance swimmers use to fend off the elements, Trudy Ederle rhythmically beat the cold, dark water. She aspired to complete the crossing "purely for the honor of it." She had no sponsors, except for her family, who spent roughly $10,000 to finance the endeavor. There was no promise of financial gain if she succeeded. An observer on the accompanying tugboat exclaimed, "She is regarded as the most perfect swimmer.... She goes through the water with a beautiful overhand stroke and crawl kick.... The whole action of the swimmer is accompanied by a minimum of efforts and of splashing." On the tugboat, a Victrola played some of her favorite music, including "Yes, We Have No Bananas," and at times Trudy even sang along.

As the sun began to set on the courageous swimmer, her trainer aboard the tugboat demanded she quit the swim. The seas had become violently rough with twenty-foot swells, and he thought her safety was more important than achieving the goal. He yelled out, "Trudy, quit!" Trudy yelled back, "What for?" Her father, also aboard the boat, knew his daughter's inner determination and paid the apprehensive tug captain a substantial sum of money to continue the journey north across the Channel. The swim continued until she finally reached British land at Kingston, nearly thirty-five miles from where she began, fourteen miles longer than the intended route. Amazed Britons were there at dusk to welcome her and honked their car horns in unison. Ederle was more than just the first woman to complete the Channel swim; her time was nearly two hours faster than the four men who had swum the Channel. She was hailed back home in the United States as a true champion. The *New York Times* sang her praises: "Gertrude Ederle has all the qualities that go to make up the kind of heroine whom America will ungrudgingly and freely worship and honor for her splendid accomplishment.... The record of her 19 years shows her to be courageous, determined, modest, sportsmanlike, generous, unaffected, and perfectly poised." Others called her "America's Best Girl." She was greeted in her home city with a ticker-tape parade, usually reserved for great teams or male heroes.

Gertrude Ederle did more for the women's rights movement in one day than many others who had gone before her. She inspired young girls to chase their dreams, athletic or otherwise. Soon after her swim, she launched a career in Vaudeville performing in an aquatic act. There she could and did capitalize on her newfound fame: earning $6,000 per week at her peak. But fame and fortune came quickly crashing down.

In 1928, two years after her great accomplishment, Ederle became deaf. An early diagnosis blamed her Channel swim for the hearing loss, as that much time in the water can damage the ears. A childhood case of the measles may also have been to blame, and some even speculated that a nervous condition acquired in the aftermath of her triumph had led to her condition. Regardless, tragedy had struck the young heroine and her future was in doubt.

In the years after becoming deaf, Ederle attempted to find a job as a swimming instructor. When this proved fruitless, she volunteered to teach deaf children to swim. Though many of her students had tried to swim previously, they had not had a teacher who, like Trudy, could identify with their hearing impairment. They fell in love with her and were inspired by her story. her instruction may have even saved lives, since drowing was a more common occurrence then, especially among deaf individuals who could not call for help.

A few years later, in 1933, Ederle fell and broke her hip. Some doctors predicted she would never walk again, but after four years she proved them wrong. And in 1939 Ederle returned to the spotlight one last time by swimming at the 1939 World's Fair in New York, prime entertainment for her hometown fans. After that, she lived a quiet life on her own. "When I went deaf, it made me very shy, and I still shy away from people," said Ederle in 1961.

Gertrude Ederle is a shining example of someone who rose to great heights, suffered a terrible setback, but ultimately struggled her way back to success. She had captured the hearts and minds of a generation yearning for female heroes. She helped to shape the future of American sports. But of all the good that can be said about her, Gertrude Ederle's best role was in showing that health setbacks cannot constrain a buoyant, energetic spirit. She died in 2003 having lived a long and fruitful life. Hers was a triumph of spirit over body, victory over defeat, and optimism over doom.

Faith Triumphant
Our hearts, our hopes, are all with thee,
Our hearts, our hopes, our prayers, our tears,
Our faith triumphant o'er our fears,
Are all with thee—are all with thee.
—Henry Wadsworth Longfellow (The Building of the Ship, 1849)

Facts of the Matter
Together with Pride

Born in 1968 in Washington, D.C., Curtis Pride was deaf from birth, as opposed to Gertrude Ederle's loss of hearing later in life. Growing up in Maryland, Pride never let his hearing impairment stand in his way. As a high school student, he graduated with a 3.6 grade point average and was a star player on the baseball, basketball and soccer teams. As a scholar-athlete at William & Mary, he played both basketball and baseball. Pride signed with the New York Mets organization in 1986 and made his major league debut in 1993 with the Montreal Expos, where he received a standing ovation on the occasion of his first professional hit, a double. Throughout a lengthy career Pride also played for the Detroit Tigers, Boston Red Sox, Atlanta Braves, New York Yankees, and the Los Angeles Angels of Anaheim.

Because he recognized the importance of hearing-impaired role models in the lives of young people who are hearing-impaired, Curtis Pride started the Together With Pride Foundation (www.togetherwithpride.org). The foundation's mission is "to support and create programs for hearing-impaired children that focus on the importance of education and the learning of life skills along with promoting a positive self esteem." Having experienced the reality of triumph in his own life and career, Pride wants young people who are hearing-impaired "to take pride in their abilities in order to achieve their goals" so that they, too, may experience the joy of victory and success.

T R U S T

Ken Venturi

In 1964, Ken Venturi was a struggling golfer on the professional tour. Earlier in his career, when he was barely twenty-five years old, Venturi had been compared to the legendary Ben Hogan. However, several close losses in the prestigious Masters Tournament made the young Venturi doubt his own talent. For four years he lapsed into relative obscurity and started to look like a has-been. He failed to qualify for tournaments in which he had once played routinely. Then something occurred that changed his life forever, making him a man who once again could trust in family, friends and himself.

❧

Ken Venturi was born in 1931 to working class parents in San Francisco, California. During the Great Depression, his father worked on the docks at the San Francisco port, but eventually landed a job managing the pro-shop at Harding Park, a local public golf course. As a fringe benefit of his father's new job, young Ken Venturi had free access to a golf course and played as often as he could. The game overtook him as a child. At age nine, he began caddying for local players, and at age thirteen he played his first full round and shot a 172.

Although he received guidance and encouragement from his father, Venturi's desire to succeed at golf came from within himself. Not only did he greatly love this cerebral sport, but on the golf course he found an escape from his troubles with his peers. Young Ken Venturi had a serious speech impediment and a quick temper. His schoolmates' constant jokes about his stuttering wore thin with Venturi. Instead of subscribing to the "sticks and stones" approach, he struck with his fists to protect his ego. In one incident, even a teacher embarrassed him in front of the entire class about his stammer. When a fellow student joined in the taunting, Ken threw a chair across the room at him, and refused to return to that teacher's class for the remainder of the school year. For Venturi, golf provided the only retreat from an otherwise painful world.

That same stubborn, combative spirit helped Venturi to overcome his humiliating speech problems. Golfing became the vehicle for his therapy; the golf course was his home away from home. In the familiar outdoor setting, striding along the lush green fairways from tee to green, he held fluid conversations with an imaginary caddy and reveled in the cheers of adoring, imaginary fans. The schoolboy tirelessly strode throughout Harding Park and taught himself to speak without a stutter.

As Venturi's speech improved, so did his golf game—dramatically. As a teenager, he played every day after school until he went to an evening job, where he squeezed in his homework assignments. This work ethic and countless hours of practice, sometimes eight or nine hours on one hole, forged his swing into a masterful stroke. He became a golf prodigy.

The proof of Venturi's well-honed golf skills came in 1948 when he won the San Francisco City Championship. The event brought out the best amateurs of all ages in his home city, known for its enthusiastic golfers. At seventeen, he was the youngest player by many years ever to win this tournament. Yet Venturi had a degree of confidence that belied his age, an underlying trust in his abilities that made him play like a winner. This confidence encouraged Venturi to attempt daring iron shots or roll putts that would make other golfers shudder. Confidence, along with a solid swing, was his greatest asset on the golf course. Off the course, his inner courage was galvanized by the disappearance of his stutter. In playing golf, Venturi unleashed a force, a determination deep within him that defied any detractors who might stand in its way. At the same time, he received his father's words of advice, words that would later seem to have been predictive: "If you win, remember that you have to keep on practicing. If you lose, all it means is that you have to work a little harder."

In the late 1940s, golf dominated Venturi's schedule as he entered San Jose State College. There he paid his own way by holding down several menial jobs. While at college, his high-caliber amateur play attracted the attention of a well-known San Francisco car dealer, Ed Lowery. Lowery, also an excellent amateur golfer, had lost his nine-teen-year-old son in World War II and was known to take a fatherly interest in area youth. In the twenty-one-year-old Venturi, Lowery saw unbridled talent and potential for lasting greatness in the sport, and he soon became his coach and mentor. He even gave Venturi a job as a car salesman.

Through Ed Lowery, Venturi met his golf idol and future coach, By-ron Nelson. Nelson, a legend of the game, had won fifty-two profession-al tournaments, including eleven in a row in 1945. Lowery took Nelson to observe Venturi's swing during a practice round. Venturi had scored a blistering 66 that day, but Nelson's response to the enthusiastic young amateur was, "There are seven or eight things you should correct. I'll meet you out here tomorrow morning." With that initial evaluation, a long and valuable relationship began.

Still in his early twenties, Venturi enjoyed a meteoric rise to the top of the amateur golf ranks and earned a spot in two illustrious interna-tional tournaments, competing against the best amateurs from Canada and Mexico. He then competed in the Walker Cup against Great Brit-ain's best in 1953. His play in both the America's Cup and the Walker Cup helped lead the United States teams to victories. He clearly had proven himself as one of the world's best amateur golfers.

#‒#

Because of his achievements, Ken Venturi received a flattering invitation early in 1956 to compete in one of professional golf's most prestigious events, the Masters Tournament. The best players from all over the world annually converge in Augusta, Georgia to vie for the honor of wearing the signature green jacket as Masters champion. Although Venturi had just completed two years of military service in Europe and had not yet won either an amateur or professional national title, sportswriters speculated that he could win this one since he possessed all the necessary weapons. Brandishing his strong, fluid swing, he struck his wood and iron shots with power and marksman-like precision. He attacked shots with confidence. When his tee or iron shots strayed, he made bold, unorthodox shots to save strokes. Venturi had an uncanny touch on and around the greens, and putting was his strength. The handsome, 6 foot, 170-pound Californian, although puzzled by the advance publicity, also wholeheartedly believed he could win the 1956 Masters.

When the tournament began on that April day, all eyes in the golfing world focused on the course at Augusta National, known for its beautiful and abundant azaleas, meticulously manicured fairways, and notoriously fast and sloping greens. It challenges golfers with its length and layout. This, combined with the pure prestige of the Masters title, set the stage for high sports drama. Even the most strident and seasoned golfers can be intimidated, let alone a twenty-four-year-old rookie, yet the young amateur was not shaken.

Venturi began the tournament with an opening round of 66 on the par-72 course, the lowest score ever by an amateur at this hallowed tournament. He followed with a second-round 69, proving that his low scoring was no fluke. As he entered the third round, he was ahead by four strokes, hotly pursued by legendary golf veterans Cary Middlecoff, Sam Snead, and Ben Hogan.

Sportswriters and spectators wondered when Venturi would wilt under the pressure. Then they witnessed him shoot a front-nine 40 in the third round. With temperatures unseasonably cold and winds gusting up to fifty miles per hour, most scores were over par that day. Venturi's third-round beginning was so uncharacteristic of his previous two rounds that it seemed his nerves had sabotaged him. Remarkably, he steadied himself on the back nine to shoot a 35 and avoided collapse. One sportswriter commented that such a recovery on the back nine under such adverse weather conditions and extreme pressure was "a combination of skill and courage." After each of the first three rounds, the young amateur reeled in the face of national press attention, phone calls, and interviews. Trying to put all those distractions behind him, Venturi looked forward to the fourth and final round of the tournament.

Leading by four strokes at the start of the final day, Venturi was mentally prepared to win. He struck the ball well, but lingering bad weather made scoring difficult. Venturi's final round of 80 would have been good enough to win except for an amazing effort by veteran Jack Burke Jr., who had started the day eight strokes behind. Burke had paid his dues on the professional golf tour, and this come-from-behind win marked his first major victory.

Venturi stood stone-faced as he watched the defending champion, Cary Middlecoff, slip the winner's green jacket on Burke. In the presentation Middlecoff said, "Even though young Ken Venturi's heart may be broken, a young heart bleeds easily but mends very fast." Sportswriters labeled the loss as a "choke," a stinging comment that later would haunt Venturi and cause him to question his ability as a player.

❧❦

With the disappointment of the 1956 Masters behind him, Venturi improved upon his already steady golf game while selling cars for Ed Lowery. But come September, he was eliminated in the first round of the U.S. Amateur Championship by someone he knew he could beat. Oddly enough, this tempted him to turn professional. By now he had a wife, Conni, two young sons, a mortgage, and no money in the bank. Ed Lowery had offered to set him up in the car business, a business that eventually would be worth a half million dollars. But the lure of the little white ball overcame the security of a steady paycheck. With his wife's blessing, Ken Venturi became a professional golfer.

Eligible to play in the 1957 U.S. Open, Venturi had an immediate impact. He finished in a respectable tie for sixth in his first major tournament as a professional, then won the top prize at tournaments in St. Paul, Minnesota, and Milwaukee, Wisconsin, and made good money in many other events. His strong showing in 1957, after being eligible for only half of the year, earned him pro golf's Rookie of the Year honors. He had begun to be compared to some of golf's all-time greats.

In 1958, Ken Venturi won four tournaments and even a new four-seat Ford Thunderbird. He had become one of golf's top money-winners. Still, a major tournament win eluded him (in professional golf, though there are many tournaments, only four are considered "major" tournaments: the Masters, the U.S. Open, the Open Championship, and the PGA Championship). The 1958 Masters ended with an exciting and close win by Arnold Palmer. Though Venturi finished in a tie for fourth, he was a mere two strokes behind Palmer at the tournament's end.

In 1960, with his game in championship form, Venturi once more set his sights on the Masters in April. But when the first round ended with Venturi shooting a 73 to Palmer's 67, the press jeeringly reminded the sporting world of Venturi's 1956 fourth-round fall to Jack Burke. Venturi commented later, "There is something inside me which, as when I was a stammering schoolboy, makes me bristle and fight like a tiger when I feel people think I can't do something." With renewed motivation, Venturi battled for the lead, and a final round of 70 put him ahead with only Arnold Palmer contesting. The charismatic Venturi came off the course to loud cheers from the gallery and an almost sure victory. Having finished the round before Palmer, Venturi only could watch and wait. He had already been fitted for the winner's green jacket.

One stroke behind Venturi, Arnold Palmer had three tough holes left to play. On the second shot of the sixteenth hole, Palmer hit the ball too hard, but by a fluke the sailing shot hit the pin, which prevented it from going over the green. He knocked in an easy two-foot putt to save par. To beat Venturi, Palmer needed two birdies in a row. On the seventeenth hole, he sank a fifty-two-foot putt for one of them. On the eighteenth hole, his approach shot fell within eight feet of the pin. Palmer buried it for the win. Venturi, not watching, knew by the roar of the crowd that his hopes had been buried by that putt. Another one-stroke loss at the Masters devastated the twenty-nine-year-old golfer. Although he earned $41,230 that year, second only to Arnold Palmer in prize money, the prize he wanted the most, a Masters title, still evaded him.

After that tough loss at Augusta in the spring of 1960, and until the middle of 1964, Ken Venturi's life slid into a period he later dubbed as his "self-pity" years. When, at the 1961 Masters one year later, Arnold Palmer double-bogeyed the eighteenth hole to give Gary Player the unexpected win, Venturi could not help but wonder why the opposite seemed to happen to him. He referred to Augusta as his "private hell, his Armageddon, mental torture," and he began to believe the negative press he received.

Adding to his growing emotional anguish, a series of physical ailments plagued Venturi. Back spasms, walking pneumonia, tendonitis in his wrist, and injuries suffered in a 1962 car accident combined to erode his spirit. His once healthy self-confidence crossed the line into stubborn pride. He refused help from his family and longtime friends Byron Nelson and Ed Lowery. Rather than look to the future, Venturi narrowed his focus on his past and was obsessed with his failures and setbacks, becoming what one sportswriter termed "an unhumble loner." The power that had been unleashed within Ken Venturi as a young man had gone astray. Mysteriously, his stuttering returned in his adulthood.

By 1963 Venturi's golf game had deteriorated fully. A nationally televised match in Las Vegas, pitting Byron Nelson and Venturi against Arnold Palmer and Gary Player, exposed to the world how completely his game had fallen apart. He was publicly humiliated and privately distraught. For the third year in a row, he failed even to qualify for golf's other highly coveted tournament, the U.S. Open. And at the Sahara Invitational, he approached the registration desk and put on a facade of confidence. When the clerk told him his name was not even on the player's list, an angered yet broken Ken Venturi turned and walked away, believing his slide into oblivion was complete.

Golf, the game that had comforted Venturi since childhood, was now torture. Alcohol replaced it as a retreat from his mounting pain. He spent fewer nights at home with his family. Instead, he ended up in local bars drinking with people who ridiculed his misfortune, sometimes sarcastically telling him he was on his way back. After a bar acquaintance called him a bum and a has-been, the one-time golf phenomenon released his fury on the man, punching him and knocking him to the ground. Venturi had to be restrained and steered out of the bar. During these years, he was ignored at San Francisco restaurants where he once had been treated like a king.

From the $41,230 Venturi earned in 1960, he dropped to about $25,000 in 1961, then to about $7,000 in 1962, and down to a paltry $3,800 in 1963. He was almost broke. As 1964 began, Venturi's marriage was at the breaking point from the pressure. To top it off, the clothing company that had once done so well with the Ken Venturi golf line notified him that they no longer wanted his endorsement, explaining that his name carried very little sales value.

Early in 1964, Venturi won $1,100 in the Pensacola Open, the first four-figure check he had won in two years. But he still routinely missed the cut at tournaments and made no money for his efforts. A story in *Sports Illustrated* portrayed Venturi as a stubborn man who refused any help. Venturi was enraged. The crowning blow to his confidence came that spring, when he failed even to receive an invitation to the 1964 Masters, a tournament in which he had played the previous eight years. He was forced to watch it on television. Not long after that disappointment, Venturi and his wife separated.

❖

Now completely alone to nurse his disappointments, Venturi was despondent. During his isolation, he once stayed up all night in his basement, slowly and deliberately polishing each of his golf clubs, which he said "no longer obeyed my will." That night, after finally reflecting on the mess he had made of his life, he felt an unusual need to pray, recognizing that "reverence was another priceless principle, along with humility, friendship, kindness, and love, which I had shunted aside in those introverted years of increasing hopelessness." Venturi asked God to give him one more chance to prove he was a man. He decided to stop drinking and deal with the problems in his golf game and in his life. The walls of protection surrounding his heart cracked, and he allowed his family and friends to re-enter.

During a practice round, his loyal friend Ed Lowery noticed a subtle flaw in Venturi's hip position during his swing. Venturi self-consciously had tried to copy Arnold Palmer's stance in order to match Palmer's long drives. Lowery convinced Venturi to position himself more squarely and swing like Ken Venturi. He had been making the mistake of "steering" the ball; now he started to hit it solidly. This slight change in his swing produced a dramatic improvement in his play.

While Venturi was restoring his stroke at home in San Francisco, he was also restoring his soul with the encouragement of a young, empathetic Catholic priest, Father Francis Kevin Murray. Venturi admitted how his hardened heart had undermined not only his natural skills as a golfer, but had shut out those he loved because of a self-induced lack of trust. He recounted how Father Murray quietly "explained life and its trials and their meanings, showed me how I was able to accept tribulations without resentment or retreat, convinced me completely that I could accomplish the things I wanted if I would think not only of myself but also of the many people who were solidly on my side, and demonstrated that I was not a lost soul living alone on a barren island."

Just as it had taken Ken Venturi many years to forge his skillful golf swing, it had taken four tumultuous years to forge a proper perspective on life. In the past, he had formed an identity based on his golfing success, and now he was building character from his response to failure. As Venturi practiced what the priest shared, his wife and two sons came back to him. With their support and a newfound peace, he decided to give professional golf one more try before he abandoned it for good.

Roughly six weeks later, after pleading with the Thunderbird Classic organizer for an invitation, Venturi played four strong rounds of golf the way he had four years earlier. He scored well enough to place him in a respectable tie for third. In the not too distant past this outcome would have disappointed the former prodigy, but the $6,250 was more than he had won in all of 1963. He called his wife and cried out of sheer joy as the tensions that had hampered his game and his life started to loosen.

When Venturi qualified for the 1964 U.S. Open for the first time in four years, Conni flew east to be with her husband. Along with the PGA, the British Open, and the Masters, the U.S. Open represents one of international golf's most coveted titles. That year it was held in suburban Washington, D.C., at the Congressional Country Club, an extremely difficult course. Now a thirty-three-year-old veteran, Ken Venturi displayed a calmness and humility that had been lacking in past tournaments. On the Wednesday night before the Open began, Ken and Conni found a nearby Catholic church and begged the priest to open it for them. Alone in the church that night, the couple prayed together. Venturi asked God "to please give me faith in myself," something he was regaining step by step.

In the opening round Thursday, Venturi played par golf, not great but steady, for a score of 72 on the par-70 course. Although nervous, Venturi had nothing to lose and approached the course with his former attacking style. To keep his outlook in the proper perspective, he went back to the same church Thursday night. This time, he asked for a sign or message that God had heard his prayers for a further boost in his growing confidence.

During the second round Friday, Venturi shot even par, another steady score. Afterward in the clubhouse, he overheard two players discussing him behind a row of lockers. One commented on how well the renewed Venturi had played so far, and the other responded with, "I sure hope it will last, but...." Venturi knew that was a reference to his reputation for "choking" in the big tournaments and wondered if he would ever shake it.

Trying to ignore that incident and remain focused, Venturi checked his mail at the club that Friday afternoon. An envelope bearing the return address of Father Murray caught his attention. As he opened the letter from his priest and friend, Ken Venturi acknowledged it as the sign he had sought in the church the night before. Six pages long, handwritten on yellow lined paper, the letter contained some helpful golf tips. But more importantly, Father Murray's words of trust in his friend's skills and character calmed and inspired Ken Venturi. Murray wrote:

> *Dear Ken,*
>
> *For you to become the U.S. Open champion would be one of the greatest things that happened during the year.... There are so many people who need the inspiration and encouragement that your winning would give them. Most people are in the midst of struggle. If not with their jobs, then it's their family life or their health or their drinking or their frustrations. For many, there is the constant temptation to give up and quit trying. Life seems to be too much and demands are too great.*
>
> *If you would win the U.S. Open, you would prove to millions of people that they can be victorious over doubt and struggle, and temptation to despair.*

To win this tournament, a man needs a number of ingredients:
true ability, strong motivation, steadiness, momentum, and faith
in yourself. And this you have in more than enough measure to do
the job. You are at peace with yourself. You respect yourself. You
are truly the new Ken Venturi, born out of suffering and turmoil,
but now wise and mature and battle-toughened.

Venturi folded up the yellow letter and placed it in his pocket. He
carried it with him everywhere for the next few weeks.

The final two rounds of the 1964 U.S. Open were played back-to-
back on Saturday. This format, an adaptation from the original British
Open, had all but disappeared from the U.S. tour, except for this tournament. Officials prided themselves on challenging golfers' skill and endurance in requiring thirty-six holes to be played in one day. Congressional Country Club, called by some players "the monster," had long,
narrow fairways, high grass in the rough and very parched greens. On
that June day near Washington, D.C., with the mercury sweltering to
near 100 degrees and the humidity in the ninety-percent range, playing
two rounds of golf became a matter of survival.

Ken Venturi had played steadily on Thursday and Friday, and he began Saturday's rounds six strokes behind the leader, but his confidence
brimmed early in the day. His ten-foot attempt at birdie on the first hole
hung on the lip of the cup for a full minute and then dropped in. Later,
he would reminisce, "When that happened, I said to myself, 'Well. Well!
If that's the way things are going, I might as well make the most of it.'" He
would go on to birdie holes 4, 5, 8, and 9, shooting a scorching 30 on the
front nine and sharing the lead with another Californian, Tommy Jacobs.

By the final two holes of the Saturday morning round, Venturi felt
the effects of the oppressive heat. He described the seventeenth green

as tilting from side to side, and by the time he reached the eighteenth green, severe dizziness made him see three holes. Had Venturi not missed the short putts of eighteen and thirty inches on these last two holes, he would have been tied for first place. As it turned out, Jacobs shot a back-nine 34 and Venturi shot a 36. But as the round ended, Venturi felt his knees buckle under worsening heat exhaustion. He nearly passed out when officials took him by car to the clubhouse, where he had only a fifty-minute rest period before the final, afternoon round began.

➤◄

Once in the clubhouse, Venturi's condition worsened and the tournament doctor warned that reentering the heat in his condition could be fatal. After less than an hour of rest, drinking tea, and taking salt tablets, a weakened Venturi insisted on playing the fourth round. The reluctant doctor agreed, only under the condition that he follow along the entire course in case Venturi went into convulsions. Venturi recalled that when he stepped up to the first tee, "just the thought of Father Murray's letter" gave him the strength to continue. Because of his condition, he could not think about what he was doing, relying instead on utter instinct. He took his driver and "cut the heart right out of the fairway with an arrow-straight drive, but... the golf course seemed to be moving toward me as I marched in place with grotesque steps."

As the afternoon wore on, the two Californians, Jacobs and Venturi, dueled for the championship. After Jacobs shot two-over-par on the third hole, they were tied for the lead. Then a majestic birdie on the 599-yard ninth hole put Venturi alone at the top. Despite his ashen appearance and his weakened legs, he struck the ball with astonishing sharpness. After losing the lead, Jacobs felt forced to gamble and scored a succession of bogeys, increasing Venturi's lead to four strokes.

Toward the end, Venturi's friends had to direct him from hole to hole and shot to shot, since he was thoroughly disoriented. Excited fans cheered him onward as he neared the finish. On the eighteenth fairway he hit a weak but straight drive, but his knees were wobbling and his head drooped from exhaustion. One of the officials strolled up close to the pale Venturi and said quietly into his ear, "Hold your head up, Ken. You're a champion now."

Taking note of his location, Venturi doffed his trademark white linen cap to acknowledge the thundering applause. Sportswriter Herbert Warren Wind of the *New Yorker* recounted the scene: "He was going to make it now, he knew, and in response to the tumultuous ovation he received as he descended the hill, he removed his cap for the first time that day. A little sun would not hurt now. I shall never forget the expression on his face as he came down the hill. It was taut with fatigue and strain, yet curiously radiant with pride and happiness."

With perspiration running down his face and the crowd of about 25,000 silent spectators gathered around the eighteenth green, Venturi sank a ten-foot par putt for the victory. The crowd erupted into wild cheers. He dropped his club, threw his arms in the air and cried aloud, "My God, I've won the Open." His playing partner, a young Raymond Floyd, with tears running down his face, retrieved the winning ball and handed it to his victorious partner with an embrace. Accepting the symbol of triumph, Venturi shed his own tears that day. His long nightmare was over. Ken Venturi was a true champion.

Writing for the *New York Times*, legendary sportswriter Arthur Daley summarized the events of that sultry summer solstice, June 21, 1964:

> *Ken Venturi's golf game fell completely apart a few years ago, but he had it totally reassembled today. He almost fell apart this morning from the debilitating heat, which turned the Congressional Country Club into a cauldron for the final two rounds of the United States Open. However, the slim Californian re-gath-*

ered his strength in the afternoon to win the most cherished prize the divot-digging sport can offer.

Venturi was so drained and exhausted at the luncheon break that his survival in the matinee session seemed as much in question as his chance of victory because he wasn't too far from heat exhaustion. He took so many salt pills that it's a wonder he did not turn into a pillar of salt like Lot's wife. By the last few holes he was walking like a feeble old man, but with a steady pace toward his goal.

It was the inner spirit that drove him on and on.

At the press conference after the tournament, Venturi gave credit for his strength to his wife and Father Murray. Later, he met up with his caddy, a man with seven children who had been a great source of optimism throughout the entire tournament. Venturi handed him a check for $1,000, making good on a bet they made at the beginning of the Open. The caddy's voice shook and his eyes got misty as he told Venturi, "I've seen a lot of them, but to me you are the greatest golfer I've ever seen in my life."

In 1964, Ken Venturi went on to win more tournaments, earning $62,500, up from $3,800 just one year before. He was named the PGA Player of the Year, elected to *Golf* magazine's All-America team, and joined an elite roster by being awarded *Sports Illustrated's* highest honor, the Sportsman of the Year Award.

Venturi would never experience winning the Masters in Augusta. In fact, the 1964 U.S. Open was the only major tournament he won during his career. But it was enough. It meant so much more by its unexpected and miraculous nature, and its ability to inspire anyone who ever had felt forgotten and beaten. Trust, trust in himself, his friends and family, and God, pushed Venturi back to the top. After his playing career ended, Ken Venturi combined his knowledge of the game, his speaking abilities, and winning personality to become a highly-regarded television commentator.

The Greatest Gift

The greatest gift that God in His bounty made in creation, and the most conformable to His goodness, and that which He prizes the most, was the freedom of the will, with which the creatures with intelligence, they all and they alone, were and are endowed.

—Dante, *The Divine Comedy: Paradiso*

Facts of the Matter
One of Three Million

As a child with a stutter, Ken Venturi endured taunts and insults. But he wasn't alone. He was one of three million Americans affected by this disability, the causes of which remain unknown.

In 1947, a young man by the name of Malcolm Fraser decided, on the basis of his own painful experience, to try to help people who stutter. The organization he began, The Stuttering Foundation of America (SFA), has for sixty years pursued these goals: "to provide the best and most up-to-date information and help available for the prevention of stuttering in young children and the most effective treatment available for teenagers and adults."

Ken Venturi, who overcame his stutter to achieve success not only in sport but also in broadcasting, was a key participant in a fundraising golf tournament for SFA in 2004, and has been spokesman for The Stuttering Foundation and National Stuttering Awareness Week. To learn more about this difficult disability and some of the efforts to overcome it, visit www.stutteringhelp.org.

UNITY

The 1980 Men's and 1998 Women's United States Olympic Hockey Teams

The Olympic Games are famous for athletes who achieve individual sports notoriety, such as Americans Jesse Owens (1936, track and field), Eric Heiden (1980, speed skating), and Picabo Street (1996, skiing). But memories of the Winter Games in 1980 and 1998 are dominated by thoughts of team successes. At those games, two American ice hockey teams accomplished the impossible. Both teams were underdogs going into their respective Games, with less experience than their strong international competition. Their teamwork, however, marked by a high degree of selflessness, made each group of players into a powerful unit. In 1980, America's men made sports history in a victory that has been dubbed "The Miracle on Ice." Then, in 1998, American women took center stage. Both teams exemplified the virtue of unity and the character it can produce.

The Olympic Games in ancient Greece were primarily tests of individual strength, stamina and fitness. Events included foot racing, wrestling and the pentathlon, a series of five track and field events. Since 1896, when the "modern" Olympic era began, the Games have kept much of the original flavor of head-to-head athleticism, but with the added dimension of team competition. Nations around the world compete against one another in team sports such as volleyball and basketball in the Summer Games, and bobsledding and ice hockey in the Winter Games. Countries put their best athletes together on national teams to vie for medals. National, as well as athletic, pride is at stake in team competition, and intense rivalries have developed over the years. One such rivalry was that of the United States versus the Soviet Union.

In any sport these in which these countries contended, an electric atmosphere pervaded each nation as well as a world wide audience.

The 1980 Winter Games in Lake Placid, New York, took place during the high point of the Cold War between the United States and the Soviet Union. The relationship between the world's two superpowers was hostile and icy, so much so that the United States boycotted the Summer Games in Moscow that same year to protest the invasion of Afghanistan by the Soviet Union. But in the Winter Games, the competitive edge favored the Soviets, especially in sports such as figure skating and ice hockey. They had dominated international ice hockey since 1960 and won gold medals in four straight Olympics. Their team was always fast, tough, and well-coached, using marksman-like passing and adept teamwork to demolish opponents. They practiced year-round, and their roster consisted of Russia's best players, whose full-time job was to win hockey games around the world. They were a team of international ice hockey veterans chiseled into the Soviet mold of iron-fisted dominance.

The formation of the U.S. team took place in a way that contrasted greatly with the Soviet method. About seven months before the 1980 Winter Games, a no-nonsense collegiate hockey coach from Minnesota named Herb Brooks began the United States team selection process. Sixty-eight players, mostly collegiate stars from the Northeast and Midwest, were invited to try out, knowing only twenty-six would survive the cut. The grueling tryouts lasted for sixty exhibition games and ended only two weeks before the Olympic Games began. The average age of the final team's players, twenty-two, made it one of the world's least experienced international sports units. Consequently, Olympic organizers seeded them seventh in an eight-team field.

What the seeding committee did not see in the Americans was the way that Brooks had united his team into a fiercely loyal, solidified band of athletes. "The self-centered people, the people who don't want to expand their thoughts, they're not going to be the real good athletes," said Brooks, who obviously felt strongly that athleticism and teamwork went hand-in-hand. He knew the challenges his team faced against the world's best hockey teams, and he urgently met that challenge with disciplined preparation. He needed players who could think as well as skate, those who would understand his system designed to combat the speed and finesse of veteran opponents. "It's a selling job," Brooks said. "When you want to push people who are living a good life in an affluent society, you have to do a selling job."

But Brooks wasn't the smooth-talking salesman type. Brooks' style was to be forceful and confrontational with his players. When they did not perform to his high expectations, he loudly and sometimes angrily disapproved. The players were accustomed to tough coaches, but Brooks redefined their understanding of the word "tough." He brought many players to the verge of quitting before he backed off. Recalled American player Mark Johnson: "I can remember times when I was so mad at him I tried to skate so hard I'd collapse, so I could say to him, 'See what you did?'"

As mad as Brooks made his players, the motivation he inspired in them proved crucial. The young Americans learned a tough lesson about what Brooks wanted of them: hard skating; smart; team-oriented play on offense; and smothering, aggressive defense. When they did not accomplish his objectives, the Americans suffered Brooks' wrath. For example, after a disappointing exhibition game, he put them back on the ice afterwards for a torturous practice session. His "nameless kids," as the press dubbed them, had good individual talent, but Brooks wanted much more—he wanted their hearts, souls, and minds melded into one on the ice. He trained them to utilize every ounce of mental, physical, and emotional energy they could muster. His tactics weren't popular with the team, but the players gradually saw them paying off. Said team member Buzz Schneider: "Brooks pats you on the back, but he always lets you know he has a knife in the other hand."

When the Winter Olympics started in February 1980, the unheralded American ice hockey team, far from perfect, continued to drill and practice hard under Brooks' watchful and unrelenting eye. In their opening game against Sweden's team, known for its quickness and experience, the Americans exhibited the kind of teamwork Brooks sought, but they lacked one thing: emotion. In the locker room between the second and third periods, with the score tied 1-1, a passionate, fiery Herb Brooks lit into his team. In a scene that Schneider described as "mayhem," Brooks told his team just how disappointed he was in their performance. They had played listlessly up to that point in the game, he told them. He singled out players who he believed weren't skating up to their potential. None escaped his criticism. Many of the players saw things differently. After all, with one period left to play the score was tied against one of the world's best teams. They all left the locker room angry; some were also humiliated and others in tears.

Early in the third period, Sweden scored to go up 2-1. The Americans kept pressure on the Swedes by skating the way Brooks knew they could. But with less than a minute left in the game, it seemed like defeat was inevitable. However, with twenty-seven seconds to go, a booming shot by Bill Baker sliced into Sweden's goal. Miraculously, the game ended in a tie. American players celebrated what they considered a moral victory—they hadn't quit when the odds were against them. Coach Brooks commented afterwards, "Maybe I've been a little too nice to some of these guys."

A focused Coach Brooks refused to allow his team to celebrate too much. He also did not let them attend news conferences where one team member might receive media attention as the "star" or "hero" of a game. There was no room for individual accolades or hype, because this group of players depended on one another. Brooks took flak in the press for this decision, but it emphasized the importance of equality and teamwork to his players.

Writers, spectators and fans who might have doubted Brooks' sincerity began to change their minds as the Americans went on a four-game winning streak, beating Czechoslovakia, Norway, Romania and West Germany before coming up against the powerful Soviet Union. Less than a month earlier, a U.S.-Soviet exhibition game left the American players defeated, both literally (the score was 10-3) and mentally. These same Soviets had even defeated a team of professional National Hockey League All-Stars. Thus far in the Olympic tournament, opponents hadn't even made a dent in this Soviet ice hockey juggernaut. A fifth straight gold medal seemed a foregone conclusion to most observers, but a gutsy performance by the "nameless kids" shocked them into reality.

The U.S. men's hockey team stunned a TV viewing audience by staying with the Soviets, stride for stride and goal for goal. The upset-minded Americans took a 4-3 lead in the third period. They did it simply by making the most of every opportunity. The go-ahead goal, scored aptly by team captain Mike Eruzione, occurred when a scrappy John Harrington stole the puck from a Soviet player behind the Soviet net. He passed it to Mark Pavelich, who in turn passed it to Eruzione, in perfect goal-scoring position. It was textbook, team-style defense converted into a brilliant offensive play, resulting in a clutch goal. Each American player made important contributions to the overall effort.

Still, ten minutes remained in the game, and the Russian Bear had awakened. The Soviets skated with renewed vigor and swarmed the young Americans, whose defense wouldn't bend or break. The Americans fully anticipated such a counterattack and repelled the Soviets whenever they approached goalie Jim Craig. The game ended with the Americans miraculously on top. The players celebrated an upset victory that ranks among the greatest moments in all of American sport. Craig, a key ingredient in the victory, skated around the ice with an American flag draped around his body. The crowd in Lake Placid roared its approval: "U.S.A., U.S.A., U.S.A." Team member Jack O'Callahan, from

Massachusetts, said: "The Americans won at Bunker Hill [against the stronger British army in the American Revolution], and the Americans won at Lake Placid."

The tournament, however, was not over. To win the gold medal, the Americans still needed to defeat Finland—a loss to Finland would have doomed the Americans to a fourth-place finish and no medal (at that time the medal round was a round-robin format, not single elimination). A less united team might not have regrouped after such an emotional, hard-fought victory, but Team U.S.A. came through, scoring three goals in the final period to defeat the scrappy and determined Finns 4-2 and capturing the gold medal. Coach Brooks finally conceded that this team was special to him: "[They] have everything I admired: the talent, the psychological makeup, the personality." They, in turn, owed their success as a well-knit team to him. "The Miracle on Ice," as their victory became known, was the product of unified, inspired effort and teamwork.

The youngest member of the 1998 U.S. Olympic women's ice hockey team was born in 1980, the year of the Miracle on Ice. That Cinderella story inspired many of the U.S. women in this first-ever Olympic competition in women's ice hockey. The media referred to them as "pioneers" on the sporting frontier. Some of the older women players had vivid memories of watching their male heroes beating the Russians in 1980. As team member Sue Merz put it, "I had the memory of that moment in the back of my head when we went out on the ice." The United States women had equally stiff competition, mainly from a powerful Canadian unit and a strong Finnish team. The fight for the first women's ice hockey gold medal would be intense. Some dreams crystallized; others dissolved.

The basis for bringing women's ice hockey to the Olympics was a sharp rise in its popularity in the United States and around the world. In the six years preceding the 1998 Olympics, the number of women ice hockey players registered in the United States grew by more than 300 percent, from 6,805 to 23,830. Women, who as young girls had to change their names and hide their long hair so they could play on the same ice as boys, could boast their own national team (since 1990) and now a premier Olympic team. "When I started out," said the U.S. national team coach, Karen Kay, "Bobby Orr [former Boston Bruins star] was my idol. Now it's Cammi [Granato] and Karyn [Bye]."

Assembling and coaching a team of mostly college and former collegiate players was the mission of head coach Ben Smith, who took the helm in July 1996. Smith, a well-respected men's Division I hockey coach at Northeastern University, initially made a bad impression on some of his female players. He obviously did not know what to expect, but after his first practice with "his women," he had nothing but praise for their hockey talent. "I'm pretty impressed [with the skating, shooting and passing]," gushed an otherwise unexcitable Smith. His quirky, quiet and philosophical approach to hockey and life caused one player to call him a "bozo" behind his back. But it took Smith less than a week to gain the respect of the entire team. Sportswriters dubbed him "the man behind the women."

Smith knew his role was to maximize Team U.S.A.'s potential by instilling teamwork and discipline. Many rigorous practices over a fifteen-month period, and the tough pre-Olympic exhibition game schedule gave Smith's American women ample opportunity to gel as a team. Though much less confrontational in style than Herb Brooks, Smith likewise demanded excellence of his capable and ambitious players. He also allowed his players to enjoy the limelight, knowing full well the historic nature of the first Olympic women's ice hockey championship.

Canada was a dominant force in international women's ice hockey. The 1998 Canadian team was stacked with veteran players. The Canadians had won four straight world championships. They were the frontrunners leading up to the Olympics. The two women's ice hockey powerhouses, Canada and the United States, played each other thirteen times in the months prior to the Olympics. The Canadians held the advantage, 7–6, in games won. But the Americans had something compelling going for them: unity, and a voracious desire to win a gold medal.

The will to defeat Canada reached its peak after one particularly stinging U.S. defeat. The Americans lost the game after having led by three goals. Canada simply played harder and tougher than the Americans. Though no body-checking is officially allowed in women's ice hockey, the U.S. versus Canada games were very physical, and the winner was often the more aggressive team. At the end of the game, Coach Smith made his team stand in the hallway outside the Canadian dressing room to listen to their hooting and wild celebration. "Right then we all just decided 'enough,'" said team member Katie King. Team USA, determined to reverse that stinging defeat, prepared to travel to Nagano, Japan, in February 1998.

While women's figure skating, men's ice hockey (hockey's "Dream Team"), and skiing took center stage in the prime time television coverage of the 1998 Olympics, the American women's hockey team began its quest for a gold medal in relative obscurity. That changed after the first game against Canada. In one of the most heated contests women's ice hockey had ever seen, Canada raced to a 4-1 lead primarily on power-play goals. The Americans had let their emotions show on the ice, leading to two body-checking penalties by the youngest member of the team, eighteen-year-old Angela Ruggiero. Down but not out, the American women answered with six straight goals in the last thirteen minutes of the game. The tables had turned in the Americans' favor. While they celebrated a rare comeback victory over their toughest opponent, the Americans knew what was to come: a rematch three nights later, this time for the gold medal.

Ever the master psychologist, Coach Smith had one more trick to use. He instructed an assistant to make a film of highlights from their previous games, with spliced excerpts from the documentary film *When We Were Kings*, which tells the story of Muhammad Ali and George Foreman's 1974 "rumble in the jungle" (Zaire, Africa), one of the great heavyweight boxing matches in history. The short movie had the desired effect upon Smith's team, which was motivated to achieve greatness and make history.

It was a tight game, just like most of the others Canada and the United States played against each other. Sarah Tueting, the U.S. goalie, made save after miraculous save, twenty-one in all, against the aggressive Canadians. Fifteen months earlier Tueting had almost given up hockey when she thought she might not be invited to try out for the national team. Smith wisely chose her to defend America's net. Meanwhile, the American women scored on a goal by Gretchen Ulion in the second period and led 1-0 going into the third period. A quick goal by Shelley Looney in the third period put even more distance between the two rivals. With just over four minutes left in the game, Canada scored to close the gap to 2-1, but was forced to remove their goalie with less than a minute left in favor of another potential scorer. With the net untended, American Sandra Whyte slid the puck forty feet into Canada's net, ensuring the American victory.

Players released the kind of emotion that had been stored up for a lifetime of playing ice hockey and dreaming of one day playing in the Olympics like their male counterparts. "I had chills," recalled A. J. Mleczko, "and it wasn't like one chill; my whole body was overcome. I won't ever be able to describe it." A more analytical Gretchen Ulion thought the turning point in the rivalry had been the previous come-from-behind win. "I think we put them on their heels a little bit with that game. We came out confident and hard-working, and it paid off." Mike Richter, the goalie of the 1998 men's Olympic hockey team, exclaimed, "You felt so good for them, the way they were just bleeding for each other to win every game."

Their lifeblood had in fact gone into the victory. Years and tears had been spent to achieve this dream. Team captain Cammi Granato, whose older brother played in the National Hockey League, said, "I wanted to play for the [Chicago] Blackhawks. My mother told me I was girl and that was a boy thing. I cried. I loved hockey just as much as the boys did." Even a deeply disappointed Canadian coach, Shannon Miller, graciously admitted, "It was a real empty feeling to lose. But when they showed Cammi Granato's face on the big screen and the medal around her neck, my feelings changed completely. I realized a gold medal was being hung around the neck of a female ice hockey player, and I couldn't believe the effect it had on me."

Coach Ben Smith put a strong group of women players together and molded them into a free-skating, unselfish, and highly motivated team. He gave them the spotlight and took little for himself. He unified them by way of his own unselfishness, and tremendous results followed. One of the scoring leaders, Katie King, reflected three months later that the U.S. victory "opened people's eyes. I think it's had a big impact on young girls. They know there's a place for them in a sport that a lot of people follow from day to day and get really excited about."

To Dwell in Unity

How good and pleasant it is
when kindred live together in unity.
—Psalm 133:1

Facts of the Matter
Teamwork Beyond the Field of Play

We are accustomed to the fact that teamwork is of great importance on the rink, the court, and the field of play. An article called "Dream Team Science," written by David Conrad for the National Cancer Institute, makes it clear that teamwork and unity are important in other fields, such as the field of biomedical research.

Throughout the twentieth century, Conrad points out, medical research became more and more individualized. But as the questions become more complex and the stakes get higher, teamwork becomes necessary. Finding solutions to problems requires the expertise of specialists from several disciplines at the same time. This has led to the formation of more and more interdisciplinary teams that, much like a hockey team, must learn how to communicate effectively so that the work can proceed for the good of all.

The team approach to biomedical research is still new and challenging. The prospect of finding, for example, a cure for cancer, is a strong motivational force, much like an Olympic gold medal. To learn more about the National Cancer Institute, visit www.cancer.gov.

WISDOM

Happy Chandler

Albert "Happy" Chandler, a hardy Kentucky politician, lived during troubled times, economically and socially. He was a United States Senator during the Great Depression and World War II and used his broad influence to overcome the main challenges that faced his generation of Americans: poverty and war. A successful elected official, he then turned his attention to Major League baseball—he had been an excellent player himself in his youth—as its commissioner. His guidance produced dramatic results that changed the face of baseball, and professional sports, forever.

⇥⇤

Albert Benjamin Chandler was born July 14, 1898, the first of Joseph and Callie Chandler's two sons, in rural Corydon, Kentucky, near Louisville. Like most of his friends, young Albert had to work hard, and he often spent twelve hours a day pitching hay, milking cows or doing myriad tasks that farming demanded. He enjoyed the work and liked to play as well, especially baseball and football. Life on the Chandler farm changed unexpectedly beginning in 1902, when Albert was four years old. That year, Albert's mother, still in her early twenties with two young, active boys, decided to leave her family in pursuit of a better life. The Chandler males, completely shocked, survived with the help of Joseph's sister, Julie, and a good neighbor, Mrs. Albert Wetzel. The experience was especially traumatic for young Albert, since his mother had actually disowned him to his face. But he put the pain behind him, choosing instead to focus on school, church and ballgames. Disaster struck again in Albert's youth when his younger brother, Robert, suffered a fatal fall from a tree limb. Though somewhat self-conscious about his feelings, Albert grieved openly over the loss of his brother. He later recalled, "It was the blackest moment of life. I have never felt more hurt or depressed."

Fortunately for Albert Chandler, he had an irrepressible spirit that overcame his boyhood tragedies. He loved to learn and did well in school. His keen memory impressed many people beyond just his teachers, and he utilized a quick, sharp wit to attract many friends. A college friend at Transylvania University in Lexington, Kentucky, dubbed Chandler, an effervescent freshman, with the nickname "Happy" because of his outgoing demeanor. The name stuck the rest of his life. Albert "Happy" Chandler quickly became a popular man about campus because of the diverse activities in which he participated—baseball, basketball, football, glee club, and theatre, to name just a few. He put his all into everything he did, a lesson that his father taught him on the farm.

Though Chandler had a booming and melodic voice, well-suited to a performing arts career, sports were his first love. As a baseball pitcher, he threw the ball with exceptional velocity, enabling him to strike out many batters. He also hit well enough that in 1919 he signed a semi-pro baseball contract with the Lexington team. The local townspeople took a liking to Chandler, in part because his pitching prowess led to Lexington wins, but also because of his country charm and manner with ordinary folks. He developed a firm handshake and a habit of looking people in the eye when he spoke. He also listened intently to what they had to say, which gave him the uncanny ability to remember their names. Sometimes many years (in some cases, twenty years) after meeting a person once, he could recall their name and something about them, such as their parents. Whether he intended it or not, Happy Chandler was becoming a politician. The fact that his university was located in Kentucky's capital city, the center of the state's political life, helped seal his fate.

As energetic and athletic as Chandler was, coaching girl's basketball at a Lexington high school during college seemed a perfect fit. Besides, he desperately needed the money. Through the job, he met many people and earned a reputation as a tough, clean, and fair-minded person. His players and fans also liked the fact that he was a winner.

Coaching and sports were but one facet of Happy Chandler's diverse life. He sang in his church's choir, often performing solos at the request of the minister, Dr. Archer Gray. Dr. Gray had befriended Chandler and told him something during Chandler's senior year that shaped the young man's thinking the rest of his life. He pulled Happy aside after a Sunday service and told him that he saw a "divine spark" in Chandler. That is, the minister observed something special inside him, a unique and spiritually active quality. Upon hearing this, Chandler felt confident that his future would "ignite" into greatness at some point. With such an assurance, he at first thought about the ministry as a career, but he then realized he had a burning desire to study law. Acceptance to Harvard, the nation's best law school, confirmed that it was the right choice, but still it was "a truly frightening decision" to leave Kentucky.

Happy Chandler, with his southern drawl, stuck out in Cambridge, Massachusetts like a sore thumb. He did well in his classes and even kept his hand in sports by scouting northeastern rivals for Centre College, a football powerhouse in his native state. His assessment of Harvard's talent led to an upset victory for Centre in 1921. He was paid for his scouting assignments, but it wasn't enough to pay the bills at Harvard. After just one year, depleted finances forced Chandler to return to Lexington. He finished his law degree at the University of Kentucky in 1924. He made ends meet financially by coaching high school football and basketball in the nearby town of Versailles, and after graduation from law school chose to set up his law practice there.

His new home and job did little to improve his meager finances, but it boosted his growing political stature. Coaching gave him an opportunity to introduce himself to local businessmen whose support he needed. He made friends quickly because of his gregarious nature. In law, his notoriety as a coach helped bring in business, but most of his cases were small. Often he would charge a mere three dollars to manage an estate or draft a mortgage, if anything. He made more money coaching, eighty dollars per month, than he did practicing law. But Chandler certainly earned more than money. He gained the respect of the Versailles community, which led to his first political appointment as commissioner of the county circuit court.

Happy Chandler became known for his honesty in Versailles. While bribery and deception were commonplace in the Kentucky legal system, Chandler never succumbed to such tactics. Judges knew his character to be impeccable. He also did not drink or smoke, and he had a strong conviction about how to manage his own—and subsequently public— finances: He insisted on operating free of debt. This carried over from his days on the farm and the simple, profound lessons that his father had passed on to him.

As tough as Chandler was on the athletic field or court, he was tougher still in the courtroom or with the public's money as commissioner. He won most of the litigation cases he handled, and he saved every penny of tax money he could. Tenacity helped him in love as well. The woman who captured his heart was Mildred Watkins, originally from Virginia, whom he courted even though she initially seemed disinterested. They married in 1925. "Rarely had I encountered a more confident, and self-assured young lady. She was outgoing, full of vim, good spirits, and excellent moral judgment," said Chandler about his betrothed.

After compiling a short but impressive record as commissioner, he felt ripe for elected office. He left nothing to chance and campaigned like a whirlwind for the Democratic nomination to the Kentucky state senate. On Election Day in 1929, he anxiously awaited two results. "So here I was in the dog days of late summer 1929 awaiting two big blessed events in my life—the outcome of my first election, and the arrival of our new child [their second, the first being a girl]. Some people probably thought I was pretty calm about it all. I had contributed just about everything I could to both events.... So what did I do? Well, I went down to George Stipp's barbershop in Versailles on election eve and got a haircut." Chandler was elected overwhelmingly in the Democratic primary and again against his Republican opponent to win a job as a state senator. Eight days later, Mildred delivered a healthy baby boy, giving Happy another reason to smile.

As a newly-elected politician, Chandler fought many battles in the Kentucky legislature, and he always took the side of his rural, "common folk" constituents, with whom he had a lot in common. They appreciated his loyalty, honesty and toughness. Two years later, in 1931, he was elected lieutenant governor of Kentucky, and in 1935 he was elected governor. Chandler credited his down-to-earth upbringing and his firsthand understanding of peoples' needs for his quick rise to the top of Kentucky's political ladder. "I grew up with folks. I thought I knew what they had in mind, and I did, too. What the average fellow had on his mind was the health and welfare and education of his children. And he did not want anybody to make it more difficult. He had enough trouble, enough difficulty, enough hard times, you know."

Governor Chandler made waves—big ones. He shook up the state budget, which was laden with $20 million in debt, by eliminating 130 state agencies. At the same time, he eliminated the sales tax that unnecessarily burdened ordinary citizens. During his tenure, he oversaw the elimination of the deficit while improving hospitals, roads and prisons. But most of all, he attacked the corruption that had invaded Kentucky politics. Bribery had become commonplace, something that Chandler could not and did not tolerate. A close adviser once told Mildred, "Happy is the only person I know of who would not be tempted by bribery." And Chandler later recalled, "He was right on that. People knew I was honest. Nobody—ever in my whole career—offered me a bribe. He would have gotten a broken nose."

In 1940, Chandler was appointed to fill the vacant seat in the U.S. Senate after the death of the Marvel M. Logan. Reelected in 1942, he played an influential role as chairman of the Military Affairs Committee during World War II, and decisions he made (secretly supporting the Manhattan project though it went against his better judgment, budget-wise) directly led to victory in the Pacific. His family (wife and four children) saw little of Happy Chandler during the war years, and on at least one occasion, while traveling via airplane to Alaska on official business, he nearly lost his life. He credited a steady-nerved pilot for avoiding an all-but-certain crash.

Before the war ended, the big league baseball owners, headed by Lee MacPhail of the New York Yankees, tapped Chandler as their commissioner after the death of Judge Kenesaw Mountain Landis. Wisely, Chandler waited until the war officially ended before taking the post. His loyalty to his country and its citizens came first. Announcing his decision to leave the Senate was "emotional and traumatic." "I developed sincere and enduring friendships with some of the noblest fellows who ever served their country," said Chandler. His Senate colleagues sang high praises and Chandler's mentor, Harry F. Byrd from Virginia, even gave him a kiss on the cheek. Within weeks of beginning his new job, baseball broiled with controversy. Sweeping change, much to the chagrin of the wealthy, protective owners, became the hallmark of Chandler's tenure as commissioner.

All the moral toughness and ethical decision-making that Chandler found necessary in politics was put to the test immediately. The Mexican baseball league began to lure American big leaguers south of the border with large contract offers. Chandler stepped in by banning renegade players from the American big leagues for five years when they chose to return. It forced a quick end to the threat, making the owners happy. But many of his later rulings as commissioner were in favor of the players, not the powerful bosses. He became known as the "players' commissioner." Decisions such as forcing the owners to offer retiring players pension plans and making sure that young prospects graduated from high school before major league teams could sign them were examples of how strongly he supported players, old and young.

Two major decisions comprise his claims to fame as commissioner—and, ironically, led to his being fired from the job. First, he banned Brooklyn Dodgers Manager Leo Durocher from baseball for one year. "An accumulation of unpleasant incidents... detrimental to baseball" led Chandler to take such a harsh measure. Durocher often made a public spectacle of himself on and off the field. On the field, he swore viciously at umpires, while off the field he had a reputation for heavy drinking, gambling, consorting with organized crime, and openly carrying on an adulterous affair. Many of the owners saw Chandler's action as heavy-handed and believed he was power hungry.

The decision for which Happy Chandler forever will be remembered is that of allowing Jackie Robinson, formerly a Negro League player, to enter the major leagues. He did so in complete and utter opposition to the owners, who unanimously voted against the signing of a black player. Branch Rickey, Brooklyn Dodgers general manager, visited Chandler after the owner's segregationist vote, and together they decided it was morally wrong to discriminate on the basis of skin color. "It wasn't my job to decide who could play baseball and who couldn't," said Chandler, reflecting on his momentous ruling. "It was my job to see that the game was played fairly and that everyone had an equal chance. I think I did that, and I think I can face my Maker with a clean conscience."

The owners seethed with anger, so from 1947, when Robinson began playing for the Dodgers, until 1951, they sought to reduce Chandler's power and influence. In July 1951, Chandler resigned as baseball commissioner. He had in effect been fired when his contract was not renewed. Though Chandler mourned the loss of his job, he could look back and see how he had directly changed for the better the sport he loved. Attendance skyrocketed, and fairness to players, white and black, prevailed. A baseball historian summed up the Chandler years by saying: "He was at heart a baseball fan, a man who wanted to take the commissioner's position off its pedestal, to humanize it, and to share himself and the game with its followers. In this he succeeded admirably.... To his credit, Chandler left the game in a stronger position than he found it... [he was] a man who used his abilities to the utmost to imbue the game he loved with fairness and stability."

Happy Chandler reintroduced himself to Kentucky politics and won back the governorship in 1955. He fulfilled his campaign promises, one of which was to build a state-of-the-art medical center in Kentucky, something the state desperately needed. He also confirmed his commitment to racial equality by defending rights of black students to attend what were then all-white school, while other southern governors did their best to enforce segregation: "I think every American must come to the realization... that we must bring about an end of segregation... in Kentucky we're making the change in the light of the Supreme Court decision [Brown vs. Board of Education, 1954]."

Chandler lived life to its fullest, literally. He made friends with presidents, Hollywood entertainers, ballplayers, coaches, and foreign dignitaries. He also counted reformed ex-convicts and other rough-and-tumble characters as his friends. Happy Chandler died June 15, 1991, and his legacy is as rich as the diversity of those he helped the most.

The Wisdom of Humility

The only wisdom we can hope to acquire
Is the wisdom of humility: humility is endless.

—T.S. Eliot (*Four Quartets*, 1940)

Facts of the Matter
Where Is Wisdom?

In the biblical book of Job, the confused and distressed Job asks, "Where then does wisdom come from?" (28:20). Happy Chandler drew upon his own native wisdom and his sense of right and wrong to make effective decisions both as a politician and as the commissioner of baseball. But all of us sometimes need to seek help with various matters. Where do we find reliable sources of wisdom?

Family and friends are usually the first in line. But in this cyber-age there are other options as well. One example is the Elder Wisdom Circle (EWC) at www.elderwisdomcircle.org. At EWC, advice-seekers can ask questions about any topic ranging from job-seeking to relationships to pets to travel, to name just a few. The advice is given by individuals over the age of sixty, and it is free. The correspondence is completely confidential and anonymous.

"The mission of our association," says the EWC, "is to promote and share elder know-how and accumulated wisdom. We also have a goal of elevating the perceived value and worth of our senior community." That two-fold mission is a model of wisdom in itself because it benefits all who participate.

DETERMINATION

Susan Butcher

DETERMINATION: Firmness of purpose.

*S*usan Butcher braved frigid temperatures and gale force winds to pursue her dream of becoming a dogsledding champion. Sheer determination prevented her from scrapping her goals after a disastrous and near-fatal accident in 1985 on the Alaskan Iditarod trail. She kept her dream alive by working toward it with all her mind, body and spirit.

❧❧

Susan Butcher was born December 26, 1954 in the city of Cambridge, Massachusetts, just outside Boston. She knew as a young girl that she wanted to be "away from the crowd." At age eight, she wrote an essay for school entitled, "I Hate the City," in which she described her desire to tear down the family house and build a log cabin in its place. Her parents gave her freedom to do things on her own. A self-described tomboy, Susan relished situations that frightened other people. During severe weather such as violent thunderstorms, for example, most of her friends remained indoors. Susan ventured outside to experience the thrill of Mother Nature's fury. She eventually began to travel to extremely remote places in her home state and beyond to satisfy her quest for excitement.

Her list of childhood interests included an all-consuming fascination with animals. Susan Butcher's parents recognized that she was more comfortable with animals, especially dogs, than she was with most humans. She appreciated the habits, companionship, instincts, and intelligence of her canine friends. She named her first dog Manganak, after a Canadian Eskimo in one of her children's books.

Dyslexia, a learning disability, made school difficult for Susan. But she excelled at hands-on learning. In high school, owning and caring for dogs quickly became her major subject. At the young age of fifteen, Butcher moved her growing family of dogs to a farm in Nova Scotia. The independence she sought had became a reality. Living away from home accelerated her learning process, which included lessons in carpentry, farming, and animal breeding.

A year later, Boulder, Colorado and the Rocky Mountains beckoned. Butcher's father lived with her stepmother, and her stepmother, knowing Susan's love for the outdoors, bought her a used dog sled, the first of many she would own. When they picked it up, Butcher immediately noticed that the seller also raised huskies. Within ten minutes, Butcher had been offered a job as a veterinary technician, as well as a place to live. The job provided a good overall experience of being around the dogs she loved, and it flamed the fire that burned inside her to discover a place where she could raise her own dogs and use them as a means of survival. She yearned for a primitive, challenging lifestyle in which she would depend on dogs "for transportation, to haul your water, to haul your wood," rather than simply own them as domestic pets. In 1973, she found such a place near Fairbanks, Alaska. "I felt at home the second I got there," said Butcher.

She thought of the place she lived in Alaska as "the most gorgeous spot on Earth," and survived the harshest winters she had yet encountered—temperatures often plunged to 70 below zero—with the help of her dogs. Butcher and her dogs became a team, totally dependant on one another as the nearest road was fifty miles away.

The Alaskan wilderness provided her not simply the fulfillment of a dream to live off the land, but also instilled in her a desire to race dogs. Dogsledding had become a competitive sport, and Butcher desired to enter the newly-created 1,157-mile race known as the Iditarod Trail Sled Dog Race, or Iditarod for short. Another goal was to build a kennel of 100 sled dogs. In 1977, she set her plan in motion by moving to Eureka, Alaska (which had a population of six at the time), where she inhabited a long abandoned gold miner's cabin. Within two years, however, money had run out, her equipment was in shambles, loneliness had taken its toll on her spirits, and she seemed as far away as ever from entering dogsledding's most prestigious race. Her sixteen dogs were well shy of the 100 earlier envisioned, but she had taught herself how to mush (drive a dog team), and the even greater lesson of how to survive in the arctic conditions.

Susan Butcher never lost hope. Help arrived in the form of Joe Redington Sr. This free-spirited man from Oklahoma had founded the Iditarod in 1973 to commemorate the 1925 "serum run," in which courageous mushers and sled dogs traveled 675 miles through a wicked snowstorm to bring diphtheria medicine to Nome, Alaska, where an epidemic of the disease was raging. Redington wanted the race to highlight the mental and physical toughness that living in Alaska demands. He saw such toughness in Butcher and put her to work in his kennel at a time when she needed money desperately. He also helped her improve her dog-breeding abilities, enabling her to once again focus on the Iditarod race. Redington observed a work ethic in Butcher that he knew was the mark of a champion. "No matter what she's doing, it doesn't take long before she can do it as good as, or better, than anyone else." She trained her dogs seventeen hours a day and knew the personalities, strengths, weaknesses, and even the individual barks of every one of the growing number of dogs she owned.

She competed in her first Iditarod in 1978, finishing nineteenth out of thirty-nine racers. But it was her forty-day trek to the top of Mt. McKinley in 1979 that solidified her confidence in her abilities. Joe Redington made the trip with Butcher, and together they gained notoriety by becoming the first teams to dogsled the notoriously windy mountain, with its gusts of over 200 miles per hour, to the top. Then, with the help of her friend and future husband, David Monson, she began to attract corporate sponsorship for her adventures. The threat of her dream failing for lack of money ended. She channeled all her energy and growing financial resources into winning the greatest challenge her profession—the Iditarod.

Susan Butcher thrived on competition. She lived to challenge others and herself on the dogsled trail. Her intense training regimen leading up to the 1979 Iditarod included mushing over 5,000 trail-miles. The result was a ninth place finish. After that she intensified her training to an astounding 7,000-plus trail-miles during each of the next six years in her quest to become Iditarod champion. She had brushes with death on at least two occasions while training. On one, her lead dog, Tekla, stubbornly disobeyed her and pulled the sled off the mountain trail she had directed it to follow. Angry about the detour, Butcher soon understood why Tekla had disobeyed: She watched as the trail they would have traveled collapsed into the river hundreds of feet below. Her most famous lead dog, Granite, once pulled Butcher and the whole dog team out from under freezing water after they fell through the ice. Both episodes showed her the extent of her dogs' instincts, loyalty and determination as they worked to help her achieve her goals. The respect and love that she extended to them could not have been any greater.

Butcher's training was paying off. She finished fifth out of more than fifty contenders in both 1980 and 1981. In 1982 she competed valiantly and finished a close second. Mother Nature herself seemed determined to oppose Butcher. At one point, she was stranded for fifty-two hours in a storm that churned up eighty-mile-per-hour winds and thirty-foot snowdrifts. She finished a respectable ninth in 1983 and second again 1984, but the top prize continued to elude her.

Back for the eighth straight year, Susan Butcher's start in the 1985 Iditarod was probably her best. She led the pack of sixty-one other dog teams at the fifth checkpoint out of twenty-five on the trail. Shortly after the brief stopover, in a dense spruce forest, a lone moose attacked

Butcher's seventeen-dog sled team. While the two thousand-pound animal was tangled in her team's leather harnesses, it stomped and kicked
her dogs. "[The moose] ran into the team, kicking and stomping and,
within probably eight seconds, had killed two dogs and injured 13 others, "said Butcher. "I held her off with an axe for about 20 minutes, and
then another musher came along and shot her." A long-shot contestant
named Libby Riddles, a fellow female musher, took the lead about halfway through the race and never relinquished it. Riddles also took the
honor that Butcher had wanted so badly—she was the first female Iditarod champion. "It hurt when Libby won," said the devastated Butcher.
"But there's more to it than that. I did not get to race the team I had been
working on for seven years. That was *my* year. That's what hurt."

The emotional pain of the freak incident did not deter Butcher, who
began to train anew. Living without television, running water, flush toi-
lets, and a bathtub meant few diversions from her singular goal to win.
Her kennel of dogs numbered nearly 100 and she literally poured her
life into each one (at the birth of each dog, she breathed into its nose
so it would know her scent). Finally, in 1986, with a new team of dogs
and a laser-like focus, Butcher achieved her lifelong ambition—she won
the Iditarod. "No one was going to beat me in 1986," she later reflected.
"I was *really* determined." In fact, her determination carried through
the next four Iditarod races, winning three and finishing second once.
Her dominance showed not only in her victories, but also in her dog-
breeding and training abilities. She often entered three different teams
of dogs, with different mushers, in the race, with her teams taking the
top finishes. She is one of only two mushers to win the Iditarod four
times. Alaskans Michael and Jayle Janecek praised her in the *Anchorage
Daily News*, saying, "She just might be the most important athlete to
come along and grace our awareness in this big ol' state."

Susan Butcher's successes captured international attention. Many,
such as the local and Native American women she met on the trail,

shared in her triumphs. They exhorted her by saying, "Do this for us." They gained strength from her wins. Butcher spoke succinctly about why she chose dogsledding in the first place: "I was born with a particular ability with animals and a particular love for them. I think that what you get from animals, and what I got from my first dog, one of my first close friends, is the security of constant love." And furthermore, "I have found something that was made for me."

In December of 2005, having retired from sled dog racing in 1994 in order to start a family, Susan Butcher faced a new battle. She was diagnosed with acute myelogenous leukemia, a cancer that attacks blood and bone marrow. "My whole life has been about challenges—I love challenges," she told reporters. "I've had the odds against me before and come through it. I'm totally goal-oriented. I'm a positive thinker, and I don't know the word 'quit.'"

Within weeks of her diagnosis, over a thousand people in Anchorage and Fairbanks registered to have tests to determine if they would be suitable bone marrow donors in an attempt to beat the disease. Butcher received a bone marrow transplant the following May. A period of remission followed, but it was all too brief. Butcher died on August 5, 2006, at the age of 51. In the Anchorage Daily News, Larry Persily wrote:

> *She fought that battle with some of the same qualities that helped her run the Iditarod—intelligence, drive, courage and humor. And tenderness—she welcomed the care and love of so many Alaskans beyond family and friends. Both she and her husband wrote more than once of the strength they drew from e-mails and other messages.*
>
> *She was inspiration to so many women that the mention seems almost cliché. The messages of the widespread and lasting*

marks she made were amazing. She changed so many live, and so many gained from her strength.

Susan Butcher followed her heart and pursued her goals with great focus and intensity. She is a prime example of how to overcome defeat with optimism, hard work, and determination. Nothing short of excellence was good enough for Susan Butcher, and her diligence was abundantly rewarded with many top awards, including the 1989 Female Athlete of the Year award. She made visits to Presidents Ronald Reagan and George H. W. Bush. She counted General Colin Powell, a fellow American Academy of Achievement member, as a friend. But no accolades could replace the overwhelming satisfaction she developed competing in one of the world's most demanding sports.

To Dare Mighty Things

Far better it is to dare mighty things, to win glorious triumphs, even though checkered by failure, than to take rank with those poor spirits who neither enjoy much nor suffer much, because they live in the gray twilight that knows not victory nor defeat.

—Theodore Roosevelt

Facts of the Matter
A Compassionate Welcome

S usan Butcher loved the Iditarod and Alaska, so it comes as no surprise that after her death Susan's family chose to honor her memory by establishing the Susan Butcher Family Center at Providence Alaska Medical Center in Anchorage.

The Center focuses on the children and families of people who have received a cancer diagnosis. Its goal is to provide support in a welcoming and compassionate environment, and to do so at no cost to the families.

For much more information about Susan Butcher and her legacy on the Iditarod trail as well in the care and treatment of cancer patients, visit www.susanbutcher.com.

MORE PRAISE FOR
THE BOOK OF SPORTS VIRTUES

In *The Book of Sports* Virtues Fritz Knapp has captured the true essence of a sports "hero."

—Ken Faulkner, M.Div, MA
Director of Pastoral Care
Virginia Commonwealth University Health System

At a time when many wonder if any good lessons can come from sports, Fritz Knapp reminds us that many have excelled in ways that have left inspiring legacies of virtue. May it inspire the next generation to fill their shoes.

—Mark Earley
President of Prison Fellowship Ministry

It is fitting that Fritz Knapp has written a book about the virtues of sports. He always plays hard, plays to win, and always extends his hand in the spirit of sportsmanship at the end of the day.

—Brice Anderson
Night Editor, *Richmond Times-Dispatch*

We can all gain something valuable from reading what Fritz Knapp has to say. I strongly recommend *The Book of Sports Virtues* to parents, teachers, coaches and anyone working with youth in any way.

—Clarke Franke
former Division I lacrosse coach
College of William & Mary

Fritz Knapp has always understood that values are built by overcoming competitive obstacles and not giving in to them.

—Joseph Mayer
former Harborfields High School basketball coach

The Book of Sports Virtues is a message that young people particular need to hear. This book delivers that message with passion.

—Phyllis Theroux
author of *The Book of Eulogies* and *Giovanni's Light*

ABOUT THE AUTHOR

❖•❖

FRITZ KNAPP graduated from the College of William & Mary in Virginia where played varsity lacrosse. He has taught and coached extensively in the Richmond area. He is currently the Executive Director of the Virginia Association of Soil & Water Conservation Districts and is the founder of Blue Sky Fund, an organization which serves at-risk students in the Richmond area. 20% of the author's royalty from sales of this book will serve at-risk students through the Blue Sky Fund.

❖•❖

Artist TOM EDWARDS is a free-lance illustrator living in Richmond Virginia. To view more of his work visit TomEdwardsStudio.com.